LEADING FROM THE BACK

STEPH HOUGHTON

with Mike Keegan

LEADING FROM THE BACK

My Journey to the Top
of Women's Football

SPHERE

SPHERE

First published in Great Britain in 2024 by Sphere

1 3 5 7 9 10 8 6 4 2

A CIP catalogue record for this book
is available from the British Library.

ISBN 978-1-4087-3437-7

Typeset in Bembo by M Rules
Printed and bound in Great Britain by
Clays Ltd, Elcograf S.p.A.

Papers used by Sphere are from well-managed forests
and other responsible sources.

Sphere
An imprint of
Little, Brown Book Group
Carmelite House
50 Victoria Embankment
London EC4Y 0DZ

An Hachette UK Company
www.hachette.co.uk

www.littlebrown.co.uk

For Mam, Dad, Stuart and my husband Stephen
I love you

THE POLE

It started with a black pole in the backyard. There was a four-foot-wide wall behind our terraced house, and a washing line. I used to spend hours and hours in there with Dad, Len, and every time I kicked the ball he'd say, 'Hit the pole, hit the pole, make sure you hit the pole.' I became obsessed with hitting that bloody pole. From the moment I could kick a ball I was trying to hit it. I asked my mam, Amanda, when I knew I'd be doing this book, what I was like as a baby. She said, 'Steph, you never used to sleep, you always wanted to be outside, you always wanted to be running around, you wanted to be involved with everything.' I think because my dad was playing semi-professional at the time, football was always going to be the sport I was going to play, and his drill was to get me to hit that pole again and again.

It was only a tiny yard, but we lived on a main road and Mam didn't want us in the front garden with all the traffic going past, and she had a point.

1

To me that yard was the Stadium of Light, where Sunderland play. I'd pretend I was Kevin Phillips, who was the star striker at the time and my favourite player.

I was born on 23 April 1988, Stephanie Jayne Houghton, and we lived in a three-bedroom house on Jamieson Terrace in a former mining village in County Durham called South Hetton. It's a working-class area and everyone there was sport mad, whether that was football, cricket or anything else. They still are. We were no different. Dad was an electrician – he still is, and I think he's going to retire next year – and Mam stayed at home to look after me and my brother Stuart, who's four years younger than me. If there are storms or bad weather and something happens to the grid or there's a fault, Dad goes out and fixes it. Aside from his football he also played cricket for the village team, so our lives revolved around sport. We'd always be around the South Hetton welfare when he was playing cricket, and all the kids would be playing five-a-side on the edge of the field.

Mam and Dad got married when they were twenty-one and had me when they were twenty-three, so they were young parents. I know everyone thinks this about their mam and dad, but they were both amazing and I had a great, happy upbringing. Mam didn't really know anything about football and still has to have the offside rule explained to her. She asked my husband, Stephen, to explain it the other day when there was a game on. I said, 'Mam, you've been watching football for twenty-five years. How can you still not know this?'

Mam really instilled the importance of hard work in us. She also made sure we were humble and nice and polite to other people. I think that might be a North-East thing. That's the kind of people we are. We work hard and we have good values. Family and community are important to us.

And if you're wondering, you pronounce it 'Hoe-ton'. That's how we say it and that's how it's meant to be said!

Mam was always looking after us. She works for the Department for Work and Pensions now, but I think she sacrificed her career to make sure me and Stuart had everything we needed, which says a lot. That's the kind of person she is. I care a lot about what other people think, maybe too much sometimes, and I'm always trying to make sure people are OK. I think I get that from my mam. She's very thoughtful, and Mam and Dad were both great for me because he was the kind of person who gave me confidence to do what I wanted to do but he was never pushy. He says he knew from early on that I was going to be good at football, but he never forced it. He was never like, 'You must play football, Steph.' It was always my choice. He just wanted me to be happy. Don't get me wrong, he loved the fact I could play, I think because at the time he was playing himself. But he always said he just wanted me to be active and do the things that I wanted to do. When I got older he would give me advice and a bit of feedback on how I'd played but when I was growing up they both just wanted me to enjoy myself.

I knew that they would always support me and, while they didn't have a lot of money, they both did whatever they could to help.

While I loved playing cricket, and could give it a whack, it was always going to be football for me. There was a lad who lived across the street from us called Karl who was two years older. He was football mad, and we used to play in each other's yards. My cousin, Amy, lived two streets away and we'd play kerby, where you try and hit the ball against the edge of the kerb. Everything was football, football, football.

Durham is a bit of a mixed bag in terms of who people support because it's near Sunderland and Newcastle. Our village was Sunderland, although my cousin, who's my best mate, is a Newcastle fan. Dad was one of seven boys and only one of my uncles is a Mag (the nickname for a Newcastle supporter). One of my other uncles, Keith, had a Sunderland season ticket and my earliest memories are of going to Roker Park, the old stadium, with him whenever I got the chance and then to the north stand when they moved to the Stadium of Light. I remember seeing the red-and-white stripes they played in for the first time – although one memory that stands out is the 1998 play-off final at Wembley when Sunderland played in their gold away tops against Charlton. We were in the cricket club, and it was absolutely packed with people watching it on television. The winner got into the Premier League, and it was a crazy, intense game that finished 4–4. I was there in my gold shirt – with Kevin Phillips's name and number 10 on the back – and it went to penalties. All thirteen were scored but then Mickey Gray missed his and we lost. I remember me and my best friend Lauren – she had her gold top on too – were absolutely devastated. I cried my eyes out. I've never been so upset over a football game even now, having lost in World Cups and Euros. We were inconsolable. But within half an hour we were both out on the street with a ball, pretending we were Phillips or Gray and taking that penalty again.

One of my other memories with Lauren is the time we were ball girls when Sunderland played Manchester United. I was obsessed with David Beckham and so when they asked us where we wanted to be I bagsied the corner because I knew he took corners and there would be a chance of me throwing the ball to him. He was literally five metres away from me during the game, I couldn't believe it. I didn't want to throw it to him – I wanted him to come and get it!

At half-time the groundsman gave us forks to go out and repair the pitch, two little kids. We thought we were very important.

I went to the local school, South Hetton Primary, and there were three girls who were into football. Me, Amy and Lauren, who's a year younger than me. We would play with the lads in the school yard. It never felt uncomfortable, but it obviously wasn't thought 'normal' for girls at the time. I just wanted to play. We had a top yard which we used to turn into a five-a-side pitch, so as soon as the bell rang we'd be sprinting out of class to get on to the top yard because if you were there first, you'd be on first. You'd need to get your team together quickly: I'd always pick Amy, and would try to get some of my lad mates to play.

The caretaker, a guy called Gary Quin, used to organise little five-a-side tournaments for us and to this day I have a lot of respect for him because he gave us girls the opportunity to be a part of that. There was never an issue because we weren't boys. For him, it probably could have been easier just to go, 'No, girls, you can't play,' but he really encouraged us to get involved, which I guess was pretty rare back then.

That then rolled into us making a school team, which I was in, so at first I was playing with the lads. When I was about eight, there started to be a bit of a pathway for girls-only teams, so we set a six-a-side team up. We would mainly play against boys' teams – it was only in actual tournaments that you would play against other girls – but I was still playing for the lads' team at school.

You didn't really get any grief from the teams that you

were playing against for being a girl. Though I can remember one game quite clearly because I'd been getting
named as substitute but this time, I was told I'd be starting,
and the lad whose place I took refused to speak to me. I
remember thinking that was a bit weird. I waited to play
out with him afterwards and he still wouldn't speak to me.
I think there may have been a few snide remarks from his
parents along the lines of 'Why is this girl playing instead of
our son?' It annoyed me, and made me determined to play
well because even at that age you want to prove a point.
I wanted to say back to them, 'This is why I'm playing.' I
remember scoring my first two goals for the school in that
game. For one I did a Cruyff turn in the box and put it
past the keeper, so I think I managed to prove the point.

I don't want to make it sound like it was difficult, though,
and that there were lots of bad experiences, because that
was one of the few times it was a problem. Some of the lads
might have got a bit jealous when they saw that I could play
but it was never a massive issue.

Because I loved Kevin Phillips, I wanted to be a striker.
Everyone wants to score goals. You always want to be
the hero, don't you? That was the case with me. I loved
Kevin and I also used to watch Michael Owen loads – I
absolutely loved him when he was playing for England
and for Liverpool. He had a soccer video out, with the old
Everton goalkeeper Neville Southall in net, and I always
remember this clip where he used to practise free kicks and

show some of the kids who were there how to do striking the ball. I used to rewind it and watch it time after time after time. My mam would be like, 'Are you watching that video again?' My parents got so bored of it they bought me a telly and a video for my room, so I could disappear into there and watch it and they could put *Coronation Street* on.

I didn't really think that I wanted to play football for a living. I just knew that I loved watching football and the feeling I got from playing it. It might be hard to believe now but I was quick back then! I was also pretty confident, and I liked to get stuck in, which probably made me stand out a bit. I was this girl who wanted to get the ball off the lads and prove people wrong.

Our team did pretty well. We never got to any cup finals, but we got to a semi with the girls' team and lost. I never forgot that feeling. I hated it. I'm a sore loser and I think when you're younger and used to winning and you lose, you absolutely fume about it.

Playing football made me feel important and I liked knowing that people were relying on me in different games. I think that's a feeling I have always had. I think I had an idea that there may be barriers along the way. There was nothing that I could see that made me think that this could be a career for me because there were no women's games on TV. It didn't feel like an option. I didn't see it on the telly, and I couldn't go and watch a women's game because there wasn't anyone near us who had a team. I wasn't really aware that there was women's football. You kind of just took it for granted that if you wanted to go to a game, you would go and watch the men. Sometimes we'd get free tickets at school to go and watch Sunderland and I'd pester Dad, who would always take me. I think if someone had asked me if I wanted to go and watch Sunderland women then I'd have definitely gone, but there just wasn't the opportunity to do that. You never got a chance to go.

Watching Sunderland at the time was great. They eventually got to the Premier League and it was harder to get tickets but any time I could go it was unreal.

The club would also come to the school and do coaching sessions, and in the summer holidays they would put on soccer schools. We were a close-knit community and all the families got on and knew each other because they would all go to the cricket club together. They would help each other out and when it came to the soccer schools there would always be a parent who would be able to take us all.

When I was ten, I ended up getting scouted at one of those schools. I almost didn't go: it was at a two-day Easter camp but most of my mates were on holiday and I didn't know whether I wanted to go on my own or not. At the last minute I decided to go and Mam, as she always did, drove me there in her red Peugeot 306 and gave me a packed lunch. The schools ran from 10 a.m. to 3 p.m. so I got out and walked over with my Sunderland kit on, which I always wore. I was a bit shy. With none of my mates there it was a bit weird, but I just concentrated on trying my best in the drills. It was a mixed camp, boys and girls, and they split us into groups. On the second day I'd kind of found my feet and was trying to impress as much as I could.

At the end of every soccer school you would get a certificate of attendance and maybe you'd get a medal. The sessions finished and I'll never forget this because I've got a picture of it in the house – Mam had arrived, and she was on the hill waiting for me. All these names were being called out apart from mine and I thought they'd forgotten me. It seemed to go on for ages and I was nearly crying. I was upset because I'd been there for two days and thought I wasn't going to get anything to show for it. Then they said: 'And the player of the camp is . . . ' and they read out my name. I couldn't believe it. I looked over at Mam and could see she was crying a little bit. I went up to collect a trophy and my certificate, and a guy came over to Mam and asked if he could speak to me.

He told her that he was from Sunderland's women's side and that they'd like me to go and train with them if I'd like to. He asked me if I wanted to go and play for Sunderland. I turned to my mam and said, 'Mam, can you take us?' She said we'd sort something out and that was that.

I remember waiting for Dad to come home and when he did, I could tell he was buzzing but he was also his usual down-to-earth self. He wanted me to keep my feet on the floor. He said, 'Look, we don't know what it's going to be like. You're going to be playing with Under 16s and it's going to be a lot. Let's just see how you get on.'

That was a great message and it set the tone for what was to come later in my career. Mam and Dad could have shouted about it from the rooftops but they've never, ever done that. And I like the fact that they've always kind of said, 'Just stay humble about it and, no matter what, keep doing what you do.' That's never changed.

It was always my obsession to play for Sunderland and this felt unreal, like a dream.

'GIRLS DON'T PLAY FOOTBALL'

It wasn't all football. School came first. Mam and Dad always drilled into me that I needed to work hard. Within our village there was a mix of people. Those who have done well for themselves and those who hadn't. My parents knew I needed a good education because it would be a struggle for me to get a job without one. They didn't really talk about university or further education; it was just expected that I did my best. They always made sure I got my homework done. It was 'Do your homework or else you're not going to go to the football.' When they say that, you make sure you get it done, don't you? I hated it at the time because all I wanted to do was get out and play but now that would be my advice to any young footballers coming through. You have to make sure you do well in your education because not only do you learn a lot, it's something to fall back on should your career not go the way you want. I often use a lot of the stuff I learned in education, and it's helped shape my career so far. You learn that you don't achieve anything without hard work and for me that's a valuable lesson.

I was relatively bright – I liked maths, although not as much as PE – but I think my brother would claim that he's more intelligent than me.

My parents had to work hard for everything they had, and we would get spoiled, but not to the extent of some people now. I mean, for me to be able to get the *Shoot* annual at Christmas, or a new football, was the best thing ever. Money was tight, just because it was only my dad that was working when we were younger. I always used to get the new Premier League ball and Dad would warn me not to bounce it on the pavement because the cover would come off. He always used to say that! So I used to have to go down to the village pitch to play with it. And I always had a Sunderland kit. Always.

After leaving primary school I went to Hetton Comprehensive, which was a bit of a shock for me. There was no football for girls and they wouldn't let us play for the lads' team. I ended up playing hockey. I was also doing athletics and tennis; I was desperate to play any sport that I could. I went from playing every day at primary school to not playing at all. The only time I got to play was when I was training with Sunderland, once, maybe twice a week. I wanted to get better all the time and it was pretty frustrating. There were a few girls from primary school who went there, and we could have had a really good team, but it never happened in all the five years I was there, which was really disappointing.

Hockey was the closest I could get to football. I played up front and would make similar runs, just with a stick in my hand. I never really felt fulfilled at secondary school. I don't know what the issue was there. One PE teacher actually told me one day that I would never play football for England. Can you believe that? That's something that has stuck with me throughout my whole career. I'll never forget that conversation. I think her view was that girls just shouldn't be playing football, which seems crazy now. We never won the teachers over and, looking back, I do feel a little bit let down by them. We asked quite often if we could set up a team and argued that there were enough of us, but it didn't happen. I think a lot of the girls who played hockey had already played football at their primary school or maybe outside. It wasn't for the want of interest, but the school just never said yes to us.

At least I got to play with Sunderland. I was so nervous before my first training session, I'm not going to lie. I remember the car journey – it was about twenty to twenty-five minutes to a place called Boldon. I was nervous and my dad was trying to talk to me, but I reckon it was one of the quietest journeys to football I ever had. It was scary, but when I think back it was a good experience. It helps to prepare you and gets you used to dealing with nerves. Sometimes things get thrown at you and you have to decide whether you are going to sink or swim. I was definitely a bit tentative, especially when I turned up and all the girls were massive. There was only one girls' team, and it was Under 16s. I was only ten and they were all miles bigger than me. But they were all amazing with me from the start. The coaches were also brilliant. They just kind of eased me in. In that first session I concentrated on trying to absorb as much information as I could. It was the first time that I'd ever been properly coached, whereas now kids get coaching from as early as four or five. I was just trying to find my feet but as soon as we started playing a game, I was OK. I was holding up the ball and doing my runs, which was fine, but I have to admit it was a pretty scary and daunting experience as a ten-year-old in the Under 16s. I had one friend there, a girl called Gemma Wilson, which made me feel a little bit more confident. We were both basically on trial and even though we were so young we knew what was at stake. You know that this is a pathway to the first team, even if the facilities are basic – an astroturf pitch and no floodlights – so you're desperate to play as well as you can. It was hard because I didn't really know any of the other girls, what runs they made, how they played, but I think it went well enough.

My mam, dad and brother had come to support me. Stuart was a bit annoying! He didn't want to be there, and I remember him moaning and saying he wanted to go home and me telling him to shut up.

When I think back the whole thing is pretty mad but after a while it started to feel more normal and I felt like I did OK. We then had to wait for a week to find out whether I was in or not.

They told us that we were going to get a letter and for me it was like the postman was Father Christmas. Every morning I'd come downstairs and ask Mam and Dad if he'd been yet. I was obsessed. Finally, the letter came. It said congratulations, and that I was in. I think my dad still has that letter now.

I remember Dad saying we would need to take it more seriously because I would now be training twice a week. It was back then that I sorted out how I was going to look when I was playing – the style I have had ever since. A high pony and a scrunchie to match the kit I was in, which was either red and white or gold when I was at Sunderland.

I like to think I was a good pupil, but I had a mischievous streak and would get into trouble every now and then. I was training twice a week and loving my football, and maybe I took my eye off the ball at school a little bit. It was nothing malicious, I just think I was finding my feet. There were so many pressures. You're growing up and you want to fit in. Your mates are going out on Friday nights and asking why you're not more girly and why you're such a tomboy. It's a difficult place to be in when you are trying to figure things out.

On the one hand I was a teenager, and I did want to do stuff with my mates. But they were doing different things than me. Going out, hanging around the streets, having a laugh. That's the last thing I needed to be doing. I needed to be in the gym, and me and my dad clashed massively. He kept telling me that I had been given this amazing chance, and if you get given something in life then you need to make the most of it. Whenever I have had injuries – and there have been a few of those – he's like, they have given you your rehab programme for a reason, get it done!

Year Nine, when I was about thirteen, was probably the standout. I got influenced by other people. I was never ex-pelled but I did get a few detentions and I remember one time they sent a letter home. I was mortified. I had one of those bunkbeds with a sofa underneath, and I was in bed one Saturday morning when Mam and Dad stormed in. One of them threw the letter on my bed. They were both raging. 'What's this?' Dad said. 'What have you been doing?' I was never one to take a backwards step and I said, 'I don't know what you're on about,' but I genuinely didn't! They told me, 'You and Amy have got these letters. What have you been doing in PE?' And I was like, 'I honestly have no idea what you are talking about!' Then it was: 'What about these nets?'

I finally twigged. We had two teachers in PE, and they liked us, but I think they were maybe a little bit jealous that me and Amy were good at sports. And they were very negative about me playing football, especially when I started with Sunderland. One was the one who told me I would never play for England.

Anyway, on one particular day in PE I didn't want to do a lot because I had training later and wanted to save myself for that. To cut a long story short, there was this big ker-fuffle and someone turned all the lights out. Because me and Amy were on the other side of the hall, messing around with some football nets, we were the last ones to run out, so when the teacher turned the lights back on we were the only two left in there. We ended up copping all the blame. I told Mam and Dad this, but they wouldn't believe me. To this day I'm adamant we didn't do anything wrong, and it still comes up in conversation even now!

Back then it felt like I was at a crossroads. I realised that it would take more than just turning up for training for me to make a career in football. I would need to put my heart and soul into it, and that meant sacrificing a lot. That's something that has followed me throughout my career, whether it's as simple as Friday nights out with my mates, birthday parties, weddings, hen dos. I still feel guilty for missing things but the people who know me understand it. They know that it's my job and that I have to stay focused on that.

I knuckled down once GCSE time hit. By then I knew I wanted to be a footballer, but if I couldn't make it the next best thing would be a PE teacher, so I would have to go to sixth form and potentially university. Because I just love sport that much, the only thing I ever wanted to do was something that revolved around it. Even then I was into the strength and conditioning side, looking at how that can help your performance, and so being a strength and conditioning coach was something else I thought of.

I ended up doing really well in my exams. Three As, five Bs and an A* – in PE, obviously. It was enough to get me into Durham Sixth Form, where I chose sports studies, biology, psychology and English language. I had to do biology because the plan was to do sports science at uni.

I did get another telling-off from my dad, mind. I got my first mobile phone and was texting a lad from another estate. I ended up using all my credit in one night – although to be fair, at the time you probably only got about ten texts a day. My dad drank with his dad and we both ended up getting grounded.

By then it was going well at Sunderland. Really well. Not long after I got my letter, they set up a centre of excellence and some more teams. I started playing for the Under 12s and before long got pushed up to the Under 14s. We didn't play as many times as they do now, and it could be frustrating. We would have to wait two to three months to play in a tournament in Warwick or somewhere. Because of that, feedback from our coaches was vital and we got plenty of that. I knew that they liked me because they told me so. There was one in particular who stands out. A guy called Ian Dipper. He did so much for my career and I can never thank him enough for the way he developed me. From a technical point of view, passing, turning, dribbling (not that I dribble that much!), all those little touches – we focused on them and I progressed really quickly because I liked to learn and I liked to take in everything. I would just do anything that anybody told me to do if I thought it was going to help.

Not that it was all plain sailing. We had a few issues with people who just couldn't accept that we had a women's team – and one incident in particular stands out.

When we were using certain training grounds you'd hear, 'It's just the fucking women on there, get them off.' At Sunderland, we could usually only get two hours on a Friday night at a place called Downhill. On this particular Friday it's freezing cold and we're on there because it's basically the cheapest time to get the pitch: everyone's playing on Saturday so there's not many people training. And it's certainly a bit rough where it was.

Dad had taken us. It was probably in November, December, so it was absolutely Baltic. Sunderland had hired the whole pitch but because one of the age groups wasn't training, we were just on half of it. My dad and all the other dads were kicking a ball about on the other half of the pitch because it was ours and obviously we'd paid for it. These lads, probably aged about sixteen or seventeen, come over; they've obviously been on the drink because it's a Friday night in Sunderland. They looked like little chavs. They're like, 'How long are yous on here for?' And our coach told them we had booked it until 9 p.m. but they were welcome to come on after we had finished. One of them started kicking off, complaining that they weren't allowed on the pitch because a bunch of girls were on it. I remember this lad saying 'Fucking girls can't play football anyway.' Our coach told them to watch us and see whether we could or not. They didn't like that and walked off towards my dad, who was still having a kickabout. They told him to give them the ball and he refused. He then told them to get off the pitch. I think it was Dad and two of the other dads, but there were quite a few of them in this gang. The next thing I knew, Dad was on the floor scrapping with these teenage lads! I was like twelve or thirteen, so I got upset, as you would. The coach took us inside, but all the other parents got involved. Dad ended up with a massive gash on his eye and I had to be driven home by one of the other parents because he had to go to hospital and the police station. One of the other dads had been on the floor fighting with them as well. I like to think we've moved on a bit since then.

After playing for the Under 12s and 14s, the first team asked me to go and play for them. I was thirteen when I made my debut and it was open age, so I was playing against fully grown women.

We were playing against Lincoln at a ground called Ferens Park, which was where a non-league team called

Durham City played. I remember being in the dressing room and putting the red-and-white stripes on for the first time, properly. I was going to play for Sunderland. It was always the dream, just to wear those stripes and to play in front of the fans. We didn't get huge crowds, but because it was Sunderland, and people in Sunderland are football-mad, we would get good support. There would always be at least a couple of hundred there.

I was named on the bench, and we were losing 2–1 when the manager said he was going to bring me on. I couldn't believe it, but I had to go and get warmed up.

It's me, at thirteen, and I am about to come on and play against adults. Women with full-time jobs, people who are thirty, who have cars and houses and mortgages, and there's little me.

I was playing up front at the time, like Kevin Phillips, and I remember just thinking, Make your runs. Straight away I got in behind a defender and latched onto a through ball that one of my teammates had put over the top. I was pretty pacey back then. Anyway, it was just me and the keeper. She came rushing off her line and I put it past her. Goal! Within five minutes of coming on for my debut I'd scored.

It's hard to put that feeling into words. I think the only way you can explain it, when the ball hits the net, is that it's one of the best feelings that you could ever have. I turned away and I was thinking, Oh my God. I've just scored for

Sunderland. My mam and dad were there as well as my grandma – my dad's mam – and my nana, mam's mam. It was a really cool day.

From then on that was pretty much me as a first-team regular. The other players were like, 'Right, you're one of us now.'

As a thirteen-year-old coming up against thirty-year-olds, I don't mind admitting that I got kicked up in the air a few times. Bloody hell. I think about it now and you just wouldn't do it these days – put someone that age in with the grown-ups. But, you know, I was really fortunate because the women were literally playing for the love of the game. These were not professionals, career footballers. It was a totally different time. These were people who would work from nine until five, then they would come straight to training. It was all because they loved playing football, and I think that helped me because there wasn't really any serious animosity.

Not that it wasn't tough. I did get a few kicks and stuff, and some of the opposition players tried to wind me up because of how young I was. They were like, 'Oi, you little bitch, you need to stop running around,' or 'Give us a chance!' That was when I was playing well. But then there were times when, if my touch was crap, my own teammates wouldn't hold back. I remember the captain telling me that I had 'a touch like a fucking elephant'. At the time, as a kid, you're a bit like, Oh my God. It's not a nice feeling and so you do everything in your power to try and make sure you never get shouted at again. It pushed me on so much and I'll be forever grateful to those who gave me stick, even if it didn't feel great at the time. Our captain, Karen, was an absolutely lovely person. She played centre-midfield and was about six foot. And she demanded a lot from us. She would call me out in training if my touch was bad. At first it made me angry. But then I actually thought, She's right – it was a bad touch. And that was how it was. I had to grow up pretty quickly if I wanted to stay in the team. I probably withdrew within myself a little bit. But you come out of it eventually, and it's not as if your team-mates are on at you the whole session. They're praising you a lot as well. It was a fine balance, but it was all part of a steep learning curve.

Despite being in the first team, it wasn't glamorous. For example, we would have weekends where maybe we would have to travel to London for a game. It's basically time off work for most of the other players, precious time off work, and they are using it to come and play football.

Some match days, we would go on the day of the game, and we would be meeting at the stadium or in a lay-by near the motorway to get picked up at about four or five in the morning. We'd all be cramped in a bus because for lots of the games we just couldn't afford to pay for hotels. If there was a bit of a bigger game, we'd be lucky enough to get a night in a Premier Inn. But even then, four of us would be in a room, which when you think about it is absolutely ridiculous. Three of us shared a double bed while somebody else was on the sofa bed. And I always used to share with my teammate Jill Scott, who you will be hearing a lot more about over the coming pages, and she's dead long. It was just mad. And you wouldn't get food provided either. We would either stop on the way down at the service station or you'd bring a packed lunch. Often my mam would make me pasta or whatever the night before to take down with me. We'd be preparing like that, and we would have to go and play someone like Arsenal, one of the best teams in the country. Everything was a bit of a struggle, and felt like you weren't giving yourself any chance to go and do something. If your preparation is not right, chances are you won't be right either and every time we played Arsenal we got absolutely battered. It wasn't for a lack of trying. Everybody played well and tried as much as they possibly could, but teams like that were just a class above.

And we were all paying for the privilege, by the way. We didn't get paid and instead we had to pay our subs which, back then, was about £250 a season. I have to thank my mam and dad for sorting that because obviously, at thirteen, I didn't really have a spare £250 knocking around.

We also didn't get any kit. No training kit or anything like that. No boots or shin pads. That was all on us. Every now and then, the kit man from the men's first team would bring over a black bin bag full of old stuff that we could split between ourselves. That was like Christmas. The best day ever! I remember coming home from training with a blue Sunderland jumper from the bin bag. I was absolutely buzzing with it. I never had it off me. That was in about 2001 so I was still only thirteen, knocking around in men's football gear. It absolutely drowned me, but I didn't care.

And all our kit was designed for men. It was really, really baggy and really long. Obviously, I was smaller than a lot of people. I was quite lanky but I was skinny, so literally it would just be hanging off me. But I never took that extra-large, baggy blue jumper off. Ever. Any pictures from back then, the chances are I am wearing it.

One of my big regrets is that I never got to play properly at the Stadium of Light and I never really met Kevin Phillips until a wedding years and years later. We did an exhibition at the Centre of Excellence once, at half-time of a game, but that was just us running around for ten minutes.

We trained at Sunderland's old training ground after the men had moved to the Academy of Light, which was this amazing new set-up. They would have had room for us there, but we trained wherever we could find a pitch, really. We didn't have a set home.

We were in the equivalent of the second division when I started, and in 2004–5 we had a really good season. I had scored fifteen goals, and in the last game we needed a win to go into the Premier League.

We were playing a team called Oldham Curzon, away. My dad and everybody had travelled down. We were losing 1–0.

My strike partner, Donna Lanighan, was probably twenty years older than me – we were a bit like Niall Quinn and Kevin Phillips, who had played together for Sunderland men's. They were like the old comedy act Little and Large and so were we. She was smaller than me – so she was more like Phillips – and I was more like Quinn, and we'd work off each other. Anyway, Donna managed to get the equaliser and I just remember the ball coming through for me and thinking I had to shoot first time. I did that, made a clean connection, and I can still see it going into the bottom corner. The next thing I knew, I was at the bottom of a massive pile-on. It was an amazing feeling.

That meant we were up – and in the top division.

THREE LIONS

I love my country. If anybody asks me what my favourite memory is or, my proudest moment, it has to be captaining England. The standout for me when I was younger was watching the European Championship in 1996. The tournament was held in England, and I remember the incredible sunny weather that summer. I was only eight, and it was when the song 'Three Lions' came out, about football coming home. I can still see myself playing in the yard and my auntie, who lived in Scotland, was there on the day England played Scotland at Wembley. She asked me if I'd like to have a little bet on the game. I was convinced we would win, and so she said that if we did she'd take me to the Metro Centre, the big shopping centre near Newcastle, and she'd buy me the England kit. I'm watching the game and it's 1–0 to England but Scotland get a penalty and all I can think about is my chances of getting the new kit going up in smoke. Anyway, the keeper, David Seaman, saved it and England went right up the other end where Gazza (Paul Gascoigne) scored that amazing volley. The next day, sure enough, we're at the Metro Centre buying the whole England kit and I was hooked from then on.

Two years later I watched Michael Owen score a wonder goal in the World Cup against Argentina in the living room with my dad and I think I've seen pretty much every men's international since then.

Being from where I am from, there's a lot of pride and patriotism across the towns and villages, especially given how close we are to the Scottish border. Everyone always says that whoever they meet in the North-East, they're so friendly and they couldn't do enough for you. I think that's right. I have the support of absolutely everybody where I am from. We're the kind of people who like to make people happy, and I think that's an English thing as well. Pretty much everyone loves football, and it unites people. I love it when we have a big tournament on and everybody's got that something in common, we're all wanting England to do well and you see the cross of St George up all over the place. I think that sense of community can sometimes get a bit lost in general life. But when it comes to sport, and not just football, everyone wants the national teams or athletes to do well.

Things were going well at Sunderland but I didn't really think I had a chance to get into the national team until

Jill Scott got selected. The manager, Mick Mulhern, had moved me back from striker to midfield by then, I think because he felt he needed a bit more legs in midfield. He played me alongside Jill. We were both quite tall and we both wanted to run. He wanted energy in the middle of the pitch, and we provided that.

Jill, who was only a year older than me, was called up and I remember thinking they must be looking at Sunderland players to come through. But I just didn't expect it would happen as quickly as it did. I thought they might just let me play a few more games for the England Under 19s, because I'd already had a call-up for them. A lot of girls played two or three years in the 19s and then made the move up.

I guess the road to England started when I was selected to go to a North-East talent camp, and they had a good look at me then. It was kind of a scouting exercise. Then they asked me to go to an England training camp. Dad said it was four hours away from us and there was no satnav back then – or if there was we didn't have it – and so we went online and printed out a route planner from an AA map and for four hours I sat in the passenger seat with this map, trying to give directions. My dad was amazing, he would drive anywhere to take me to wherever. I was there for about two days but my dad obviously went home. So that was the first time I'd really been away from home as well. Everything was a blur. I couldn't even tell you if I did well, but I guess I did because the next minute I got put on standby for an Under 17s camp in Ireland. But it was while I was away skiing with school. Sure enough, two days into the trip I got called up – only they were in Ireland and I was in Austria. This sums my dad up: he drove from our house in the North-East all the way down to Dover to meet me after we arrived on the ferry on the way back. That's a seven-hour, 342-mile trip. He then dropped me off at Heathrow for the flight to Ireland and drove back home to the North-East. Incredible.

From there I went to the 19s but the first team happened so quickly. I had just got home from sixth form, and Mam and Dad were with me when the phone rang. It was the player admin. England were playing a friendly against Germany and they asked me if I would be able to come. I was like, 'Well, yeah, of course I'm able to come!' The admin apologised because normally you get a letter with all the information but they didn't have time to send it, so they were going to text it to my dad.

My dad, as he always does, started sorting out the logistics while my mam packed a bag. I was sixteen and going to play for England!

I was on the bench, obviously, but I went out onto the pitch and stood with the team as they played the national anthem. I'd done it before at the younger age levels but this time it felt different. I had goosebumps.

Germany beat us 5–1 and I didn't get on the pitch. I remember watching it and thinking, This is a different level. The Germans were incredible. As soon as the game started, they just took control. The England manager, Hope Powell, wasn't at the game – her assistant took it – which was a shame, but I don't think it would have made a difference. Germany were unstoppable. They had so many unbelievable players and they were the team that everybody wanted to emulate and to beat as well. I was on the sideline, feeling a bit starstruck. I saw these German players playing and also saw our players playing and I was like, 'Oh my God, these people are actually my teammates.' Rachel Yankey was in *Bend It Like Beckham*! You know what I mean? You're actually sharing a changing room with these people, and they couldn't be any more welcoming. Faye White was captain at the time and literally the first moment she saw me she put her arm around me and was just like, 'Enjoy every minute, take it all in.' Rachel Yankey is such a good personality, she's so funny, she was great. Sometimes I couldn't really read her, but she's probably one of the nicest people you'll ever meet. And Kelly Smith was Kelly Smith. She was so quiet off the pitch. But when she came on the pitch, she was so demanding and just set the standard. So I learned from different people, even if the game was one to forget.

I also got my England gear! Again, it was massive, but at least it was new and it was mine.

Not long after, I was called up again, this time for a match against Russia in Milton Keynes. My dad and one of his workmates came down for it. We had a mini camp and played three games in nine days. I was on the bench again, but after about seventy minutes Hope told us to go and get warmed up. I was thinking, Oh my God, she's going to throw me on and there are so many people watching this game at this ground. It was at right-back because Lindsay Johnson, who normally played there, was injured. Hope was just like, 'Steph, I'm going to try you there – just enjoy it, do what you need to do, you'll be fine.' So that was me making my England debut at right-back even though I was playing midfield for Sunderland. It was a bit mad, really, and it was difficult to adjust. The feeling when I came on was unbelievable, but I just wanted to stay calm and keep things simple. Make sure I was doing what everyone else was telling me to do because there were some amazing people on that pitch who knew what they were doing. Also, because we were winning by such a big margin by the time I got on, it helped me settle in. Hope was really good in the sense of knowing when to use me and when to introduce me into that environment because I was really new to the squad. She was keen to see me at right-back and I thought it might be a good thing to be able to play a few positions because it would give me more chance of keeping my place.

Football was going well and I got the young player of the season award that year, which was crazy. But it wasn't life changing. With the England set-up then, you didn't get a contract, there was no salary to speak of and all you got was travel expenses.

But it was pretty cool to go back into sixth form with everyone knowing I had played for England – I can't lie! I think my studies suffered a little, but it was a lot different than secondary school. The teachers there loved it. They still love it now, to be honest. They were really helpful too. My grades probably dipped because I was away every four or five weeks, missing two weeks at a time, which is a lot for A levels, because it's much harder. I was lucky to come away with my A levels when I'd finished, given all the disruption.

By now, my mind was made up that I wanted a career in football and nothing else. When I first got called up for England, that was a moment where I was like, 'I want to do this. I want to be part of this.' It makes you feel unbelievable, wearing the England badge, and I wanted to do whatever it took to make sure I kept that shirt and stayed in the squad.

When you played for England, you got a training programme – exercises and drills to do on your own – because at the time you'd still only be training a couple of times a week with your club. Germany were training more than us, they were doing more than us, and that's why they were the best in the world. We were well behind them, and the only thing that we could control was fitness. I always remember – this was a moment that probably changed my career for ever – I got the England programme through the post and it said that on the days when you're not training you must do four four-minute runs. My dad said, 'Right, you need to do this, Steph,' and I refused. He was furious. Asking me if I wanted to play for England or not. He made the point that if I didn't do it someone else would – and they would end up in the squad with my place.

My brother, who had stopped being annoying by this stage, said he would come out and run with me. He wasn't into football, which was weird given where we're from. But he was really athletic and started playing rugby league, which was *really* weird because hardly anyone plays that in the North-East.

I finished sixth form college and went to university on an FA development programme. The idea was that they would get the best young players in all of England to be the face of Loughborough University. We would follow a full-time training programme and study at the same time; we'd all be on different courses, whatever we wanted to do. We didn't really get any money, so I had to rely on Mam and Dad – again – although to try and save up some money the summer before I went, Dad made me walk around the retail park near us and hand my CV in to absolutely every shop on there. I hated it. I begged him to go in instead. I think about two shops out of forty called me back, which was pretty embarrassing.

I ended up with a job in a store called Sports Soccer. I worked the delivery shift from 7 to 11 a.m. on a Saturday or Thursday nights 5 to 8. I was literally just sorting clothes out as they came in, hanging them up, maybe going behind the tills if I was lucky. Sometimes on a Saturday I would get up at 6 a.m., go to work for four hours and then maybe if we had Arsenal away, I would meet the bus later in the afternoon and travel all the way down to London and I'd only get about £20 for my troubles. And because I had so much football, sometimes I was only doing one shift a month. My pay packet would land and my mam would ask me how much I got. I'd tell her: £20. It came to the point where there was no point in really even going in.

It was important that I worked – it was the principle of it – but my mam and dad pretty much funded a lot of my time at university. And I had to get a student loan, to cover petrol and stuff. I have paid that back now, finally, thank God. I'm showing my age now.

I had actually had the chance to go to Loughborough when I was sixteen. So before sixth form. We went down and looked around, and to be honest, I just didn't really feel ready to go and live away from home at that age. At the time I wasn't driving, either. I was still playing for Sunderland, and I just didn't think it was the right move.

When I agreed to go, Sunderland were not doing well, even if me and Jill were. It looked as though we were going to get relegated. The 2007 World Cup was coming up and I was worried about my chances of getting into the squad.

Quite a few clubs were interested in me. Arsenal were probably the biggest but I knew I wouldn't be guaranteed playing time. Mix that in with going to Loughborough and I just wouldn't have been able to train with them as much as they would have liked me to. Everton were also keen and I was really, really close to going there. Mo Marley, who was my coach at 19s, was manager there and I knew she really rated me. But there was no financial assistance in terms of travel, to get me there from Loughborough.

Leeds, who were in the top division, came in, and I knew I would probably get to play a lot and the geography – a scoot up the M1 – was a lot more straightforward.

It was an exciting time of my life and I can remember going into that summer really looking forward to what was to come. There was a World Cup coming up, a new club to play for and a life away from home for the first time.

HEARTBREAK

I never, ever thought that I would get selected for the 2007 World Cup. Obviously, it was my England debut season and I had played a few times, but I thought I was a long shot at best. Hope Powell had showed that she liked me, but I thought I was too inexperienced to make it. There was a squad of thirty players that she had to trim down, so the chances of me getting picked were really slim.

We had a final England camp, which I was invited to, and we did fitness testing. We were told that we needed to be as fit as we could possibly be. I was young and I was quite fit anyway, it kind of came quite naturally. We had an in-house game and I'd played well at right-back, and I realised there was probably three of us really fighting for the same position. Alex Scott was the first choice, then a girl called Lindsay Johnson who played for Everton, and me. Lindsay could play centre-back and right-back, so I thought that she was probably going to go because she was versatile and had a lot more experience than me.

So anyway, it comes to a couple of weeks before the team were due to go out to China for the tournament, and Hope rings. She always used to start by saying your name. So she says, 'Steph Houghton'. She asked if I was OK and then got straight to the point. 'Right,' she said, 'I'm going to take you. I need you to be on it, I need you to be ready. I'm going to take you, but nothing changes.' Hope wanted me to carry on doing what I was doing.

Hope always had a way of making sure that you respected her. How she spoke to you: it wasn't intimidating, but it was pretty powerful. I'm nineteen and there's this absolute legend of the women's game on the phone to me. She was telling me that I was in because I was quick and that she thought I had something. I can't tell you how amazing that was to hear. Then it was down to business. She told me that I was going to get a fitness programme and that she needed me to follow it because we were going to go in July.

Me and Jill, who was also in the squad, ended up training at Gateshead College, which had a great gym. We'd also do sessions on the pitch with Julie Twaddle, although there was one day when Julie had us doing running sessions for two hours before realising she had messed it up. It's a bit more professional now! We both threw ourselves into it. We were doing everything we could to try and get the extra 1 per cent, with protein shakes, diets – I swear we were drinking bloody baby milk at one point.

We both pushed each other on, which was great. I first met Jill back at the Centre of Excellence trials at Sunderland and we have been friends ever since. I remember she was just so bubbly. That's probably my first ever memory of Jill, her making someone laugh, and I think when you see someone like that, it settles you down. Ever since then, all the best things that have happened to me in football have been when Jill has been there. It's nice that we started at Sunderland together, we've played for England together and we both went to Man City. When we signed for Man City, I told her we were destined to play on the same team for so long, and to have that many memories with her is pretty unique.

I guess you'd say it's a strange relationship because we are total opposites. I'm organised. I know what I'm doing. I'm probably a bit more, maybe not emotional, but logical. Whereas Jill is so off the cuff – she's been like that for the whole of our career together. The funny thing is that our parents would bump into each other on nights out and we'd get selfies of them out together in some random pub in Sunderland, having better social lives than us. You couldn't get a nicer family than Jill's. I think that's why we got on so well. We have kind of the same morals and we've been brought up in a certain way. And I just think that's a general North-East thing, to be honest.

*

Eventually it was time for our final gym session, so we went to Gateshead College. I'd done my weights and had started to plan the next day in my head. I was going to finish training and go home and pack, and then have a day to just spend with my family.

We were doing plyometric exercises to build muscle power. We were jumping over hurdles and I did my first set absolutely fine.

Then, on the second set, I clipped the top of a hurdle. As I landed my ankle rolled. I'd never felt pain like it. I was screaming in agony, crumpled on the floor. This was two days before I was meant to fly out to China, literally the last exercise of my last session after six weeks of intensive training.

I got rushed to hospital. I thought I'd broken my ankle. My mam and dad met us there. I was in so much pain, but my first thought was that I'd let everyone down. They were going to be so upset. They all thought I was going to go to the World Cup and now there was no chance. I'd worked so hard and they'd all supported me, and now it was ruined.

I had a scan and they found that I had a spiral fracture of my fibula. What are the chances of that? They are so rare, and usually the result of some major trauma or accident. I would have been the youngest player to go to a World Cup and instead I was in a hospital bed in the Royal Victoria Infirmary in Newcastle. My emotions were all over the place.

When the doctor came in and told me, I cried my eyes out. Mam and Dad didn't. I think they were trying to hold their emotions in because they knew it wasn't just that I'd broken my leg. There was a lot more riding on it. The fact that I was moving clubs, I was going to university, I was going to miss a World Cup that they knew I'd been working so hard for. There were just so many things that came into it.

I was on a general ward. Literally hours earlier I'd been getting ready to go to a World Cup and now I was in a bed next to a load of random people I didn't know. There was one old lady next to me, bless her, and she was snoring really loudly all night. They had to force my leg into a cast and put my bone in position to make sure it sat there. I was in agony and on gas. I just wanted to get home. I was desperate to get out of there.

Eventually, they took the cast off and told me I would be in a boot for six weeks. That was that. Hope had heard what had happened and she called. Word gets around quick. Dream over.

As I got older, I got better at dealing with adversity and I've always tried to get on with the next challenge, which in this case was getting back to fitness. But it was a rough month. My grandad, Dad's dad, wasn't very well at the time and he ended up passing away a couple of weeks later. He had lung cancer. He had worked in the mines, and lots of the miners ended up dying from the same illness. He used to drink a lot and smoke a lot. That's just what they used to do. I suppose it was no wonder that he was going to end up with lung cancer but that didn't make it any easier.

If there was any positive with the injury it was that I managed to spend some time with him in his final days. I'd like to think it helped Grandma. She was so into my football, and she absolutely loved it. She loved coming to all my games and kept all the programmes, and used to brag about me to everybody who would listen – she still does that now. To be there for her I think was helpful. After Grandad passed away the World Cup started, and I would go around and sit in his seat and watch the games with Grandma. I was sat there thinking, That could have been me, out there playing. And then you think, Why me? Why did it happen to me? You've worked so hard to get here. It's not very often that Hope Powell gives young players that kind of chance to go to major tournaments and she really took a risk on me.

I'd never take it out on anyone, but you do get a bit jealous. I was absolutely gutted that I wasn't there, and I was jealous of the girls being able to play in a World Cup, but it didn't mean I didn't support them. I just wanted to be there so much. I knew my role would have been limited even if I had gone, but the type of person I am, I always want to help. Whether that's being on the sideline or being a good teammate or being able to come on the pitch and do something. I don't mind. Maybe I'd have got one or two appearances, but the whole experience would have been crazy. I think in general it is just more about the fact that you're going to the World Cup and then you're not. I was only young, but it was a dream to play at a major tournament for England. That was the one thing I wanted to do, but the situation with Grandad did give me perspective.

When I look back, it was probably a lot for a kid to deal with, but I like to think there is a reason for everything. Whether that was for me to be there for my grandad's final few days, I don't really know. England lost 3–0 to the US in the quarter-finals, which was another disappointment.

The FA helped with my rehab and I would go to see the physio twice a week. I was still training, just with the boot on. And then when I moved to Loughborough, I was nearly out of the boot. In terms of timing and being looked after, it couldn't have gone better. I was back on the pitch within three months, which was pretty good. I've spent most of my career trying to see the positives in different situations and trying to come out a bit stronger. I think that injury was the start of having that mindset.

I also had a new challenge to focus on with Leeds, which was a step up from Sunderland. It was more professional, with better players. We had the likes of Sue Smith, who was a regular in the England side, a big name. To be able to learn from her and to be part of her team, and to know that I got on with her so well at England as well, made the move a little bit easier.

Another big step forwards was that I could stop paying subs! This was also when I started to get a bit of money. It was only £50 a game, but for me that was massive. I was on a student loan, so to get £50 and my travel expenses, and potentially a bonus when we won, which was about £20, was huge. I could have gone to Arsenal and got £100 or £125 a game, but it just wasn't realistic. I would have had to have moved to London and I wouldn't have settled in as quickly as I did at Leeds. It probably sounds weird, but I knew at some point I was always going to move to Arsenal – it was just a matter of time.

By the time I started at Leeds I had my first car, an N-reg Clio. No power steering! I got it off my grandad, which says a lot about the family, but it was the heaviest thing ever.

I'd be at uni from Monday to Friday, and then you'd obviously get the weekend off. So if we had games on a Sunday, I'd literally go home to the North-East on the Friday and travel down to Leeds on Sunday, then back to Loughborough that night. Sometimes during the week the manager would want us to come in for training. Fortunately there were three or four of us from Leeds at uni, so we would take it in turns to drive. It was tough, we were training 7 p.m. until 9 p.m. and then we'd train again in the morning. It was a pretty intense time.

It was also a different time. We would go out on Fridays and get absolutely bladdered, knowing that we were playing on the Sunday. A Smirnoff Ice or some kind of fruity cider was always my drink of choice. At Leeds I'd go to my mate Sophie's on Saturday sometimes, and our pre-match meal would be a Chinese takeaway! There was hardly any advice, and you did what you normally would do in life, but the difference was you would then go and play football. When we were travelling away, we'd stop at the motorway services and I'd have a tuna sandwich, a packet of salt and vinegar Discos and a fizzy Lucozade. The game has massively moved on, but we didn't really know any different back then.

HEARTBREAK PART II

I didn't have to wait long to play in an overseas tournament for England. In 2008 the Under 20s World Cup was held in Chile and I was selected. It ended up being one of my favourite experiences. Hope didn't want to throw me back into the first team straight away because I needed to get back into a rhythm and to get some games under my belt. She was quite conscious that I was still young, with time on my side, and so she just wanted me to go and play. And I had a chance to go and play every single game in a tournament.

We went out there economy class, all the way to Chile. It was the first time I'd played centre-half for England. I was supposed to play right-back but one of the centre-halfs got injured and Mo Marley, who was manager, made the switch. She put me at left-sided centre-back and told me to enjoy it and do what I normally do.

I actually found it easier than right-back. You can see absolutely everything in front of you and your body position can be quite open. I could make a lot more longer passes and I love heading the ball – and there was a lot more of that. When I wasn't hitting the ball against the pole in the backyard, Dad made me practise headers. It probably sounds weird, but I actually like the feeling of connecting with the ball. At the time, Jody Craddock was a centre-half with Sunderland's men's team and he used to love heading the ball. I used to think it looked amazing, and I wanted to try and emulate him. And there was the element of trying to prove people wrong, because some people think girls can't head the ball. I wanted to make sure I could.

I knew that Hope was watching the games in Chile, so I really tried to impress. We got knocked out in the quarter-finals, but I played well and when I came back I got myself back into the England first team for the Cyprus Cup, an invitational tournament. Hope played me left-side centre-half because Faye White was injured, and Anita Asante played at centre-back. I loved playing with Anita, she was so calm and composed. We won the Cyprus Cup and I played really well again. Hope actually pulled me to one side to tell me how well I'd done. She told me to just keep doing what I was doing, and to work hard on my game. That felt huge for me. It was March 2009 and I was beginning to think about the Euros that summer. It would be another chance to play for England in a major tournament for the first time. And then it happened again.

*

It was an away game for Leeds. Even now, I can't remember who it was against. It was out west somewhere, Bristol maybe, or Cardiff. I was bombing forward, as I often did playing midfield, and I remember Sue Smith having the ball on the wing. I made a run into the box and the ball came. I was thinking about where I was going to place my shot and then this girl just came straight through the side of my knee. I heard a massive *pop*. She kind of scissored my leg. My knee got stuck and pain shot through it. It was horrific. I was so far from home and in agony. I got carried off thinking, Oh my God, this is bad. I looked down at my knee: it had blown up massively. A mate phoned my mam and dad to tell them I was in a bad way, and to ask them to meet me when we got back to Leeds.

I had to get back on the team bus, which wasn't pleasant. My parents were also going through a rough time in their marriage and weren't speaking at the time, but they put that to one side, jumped in the car and headed down.

I got to Leeds and it was a case of getting a scan as quickly as possible. It was a Friday afternoon when I got the results, and the doctor was just really matter of fact, as I guess they have to be. She told me it was my ACL, my meniscus, and that I needed to go and see a consultant. I asked her what that meant exactly. She told me straight: 'Steph – you're not going to the Euros.'

This was April, just before I turned twenty-one, and I knew I probably would have been going to go to the Euros.

There was more certainty than for the World Cup because I could play anywhere across the back four now.

When I got the news, I was in my bedroom. I didn't even cry. I just remember thinking, Why does nobody want me to go to a tournament? It sounds silly, but the experience was something that scarred me. Because it had now happened twice, further down the line in my career when it came close to tournament time I'd start to get a bit panicky. Because you're kind of waiting. You're wondering if you can stay fit. It's almost like PTSD. You get to February, March and you're like, Come on, just make it through these months. Instead of relaxing and thinking about getting selected you're worried: Can I actually stay fit this time?

When I missed the World Cup there was Grandad's illness and this time there was something else to deal with – my parents getting divorced.

It was tough then, and to be honest it's still tough now. For me, my whole life has been about family and making sure everybody's together and everybody's happy, so Mam and Dad splitting up was pretty difficult to deal with.

I think me and my brother probably had a little bit of an inkling that it was going to happen. And to this day I hate the fact that Stuart was by himself, because at the time he was around seventeen and there on his own while I was at Loughborough. I remember phone calls with my brother telling me what's happening at home. I was at uni, so not really bearing the brunt of it like he was. I found it hard because I couldn't really protect him, and he was getting a lot of what was happening to deal with on his own. Of course, your mam and dad give you their side and different information, which was the hardest thing to cope with.

I would never want either of them to think that we love them any differently because of what happened, but it was hard. I will never forget them telling us that it was what they had decided to do, and it was tough because you want your parents to be happy together, but I knew it was the right thing because they couldn't go on like that any more.

They just weren't getting on as well. And I think because me and Stu were older, they each wanted to do their own stuff and live their lives a little bit. They married at the age of twenty-one and so for a lot of their lives they were dedicated to providing for me and my brother. I think they just got to a stage where they wanted different things.

At the time it was very, very awkward as well, because I was travelling backwards and forwards with football and uni, and so I'd have to make a decision when I had time to come home whether I would go to Mam's or whether I'd go to Dad's. Sometimes I still get that now, in the sense that I don't want to upset either of them. You can't be seen to be playing favourites because there isn't a favourite, but me and my brother have had to ride through that quite a lot.

It was tough because you're not only trying to

concentrate on trying to get picked, trying to get selected, trying to get back fit from an ACL, but you're also having to deal with your parents splitting up.

The last few years it's been a lot more amicable, because it has had to be, but that doesn't change what we went through. When your parents are together everything is a lot easier. We did try and keep them together. We asked them to maybe have a little bit of a break, see how it goes and maybe get back together – not just for the sake of us, but for them as well. We made the point that they had worked so hard to get the house that they had – we'd moved to a new place by then – and that they'd brought us up amazingly, so it would be a shame to let that go. We told them that they had done absolutely everything for us and asked them to find a way through it.

But it was just in one ear and out the other. One of them would try and then the other one wouldn't, and it was like, Well, he didn't do that or she didn't do that. And then it just got to the point where we were like, OK, this isn't going to work. It's causing us even more stress than it is them.

Because we were in such a close-knit village, it was rare that people got a divorce. I think it's probably a little bit more common in the world we live in now. It happens and people are able to go, 'Actually, no, I want to do something new,' or whatever it might be. I do get a bit anxious, and I worry about people, and I worried about my mam. I knew that my dad would always be OK because he's very motivated and he's very, I suppose you'd say, sure of himself. But I did worry about my mam a lot. She was the one that was moving to a new place, a couple of villages over. She needed to settle into her house; my brother was there one week, he wasn't the next. There were a few months where it probably affected me more than I realised at the time. But football was my release. Being able to do that and to be around different people, away from it, even though it was harsh on my brother, was the best scenario for me.

My parents couldn't work together as a team, but they still gave and continue to give Stuart and me the love and support that we need. It was just a messy few years.

When I speak about it, I do get a little bit emotional, because I love them so much, but I know it was the right decision in the end.

ARSENAL

I really enjoyed my time at Leeds and we got to the FA Cup final in 2008. As a bunch of girls, they were so funny and the team spirit was really good. The manager, Rick Passmoor, had a very effective way of playing that suited us all. We were really well drilled. His temperament was a little bit up and down – he would fly off the handle sometimes – but that was what it was like, and I don't think it did us any harm. He was just a bit of a different personality to previous managers like Hope Powell, who was always quite calm and collected.

Getting to that FA Cup Final at Nottingham Forest's ground was a great achievement. The crowd was nearly twenty-five thousand. We got absolutely battered by Arsenal 4–1, but the player of the match was our goalkeeper, Carly Telford, which I think says it all. It was so hot and to be honest, I don't think we ever expected to win, but to be there was just amazing. That was probably one of my first experiences of playing in a high-pressure environment where there's something on the line, which was pretty crazy.

When I graduated from uni, I thought we were on the verge of something. But in 2010 the FA announced that they were going to launch the Women's Super League the following season and there was a list of criteria attached, should your team want to be a member of it. Had Leeds been involved I reckon we'd have had a great season and maybe finished second. Maybe the year after we'd have won it. The likes of Ellen White had joined, and Laura Bassett. There was me, as well as a girl called Jade Moore. Then there was Sue Smith, Jess Clarke. So all these people are in the England set-up, all playing for the same team. We also had Carly in goal. So we had experience as well as youth. We had players who were able to compete at a high level and we'd been together for three years. But the rules stated that we had to be associated to a football club and unfortunately we weren't. We were called Leeds Carnegie and we were effectively funded by the university. Leeds United, at the time, didn't want to buy in, which was devastating.

I got a 2:1 in sports science but had nobody to play for. I've already said that I'm a believer in things happening for a reason, and before long Arsenal were on the phone. At the time I didn't have an agent, so they were literally coming direct to me. Everton and Chelsea were also interested. It was the talk of the village! People would come up to me and ask me what I was going to do, which was a new one.

I had the pick of clubs, and my dad was like, 'Let's go and have a look at all of them. Let's speak to all the managers. Let's go and see what it would be like at each.'

At Everton and Chelsea, I was guaranteed to play. I went to Everton and Mo Marley was a big pull but something didn't seem right. I couldn't really put my finger on it, but I wanted to be at the most professional club I could be at to give it my best shot. I went down to Chelsea and Matt Beard, who is the Liverpool manager now, was manager there. I saw their training ground and was really impressed. We actually did Chelsea and Arsenal in two days because it just made sense to do it that way. At Chelsea, they were doing some really good things and were training at Cobham, where the men trained, which was this amazing facility. Like, scary amazing. I knew it would be a great club to play for. But I couldn't get rid of the feeling at the back of my mind that it was always going to be Arsenal. I just couldn't turn them down again.

It was a man called Vic Akers who was on the phone from them. He was already an absolute legend of the women's game and played a huge part in getting it to where it is now. Arsenal were such a huge name in women's football, but it wasn't just that. So many of my England teammates were there; most of the England starting eleven was Arsenal – Faye White, Rachel Yankey, Katie Chapman – as well as other internationals: Jayne Ludlow and Emma Byrne. They were all playing for their countries because they were playing for the best team in the league. They were competing in the Champions League and had won it in 2007. Playing with those players every single day was only ever going to make me a better player. I knew that I potentially might not play at Arsenal, but I needed to take that chance.

I spoke to Hope because I wanted her to know that my ambition was to be a regular starter for England, and I wanted her to tell me what she thought I needed to get there. Her main thing was that she wanted me training with good players every single day. I asked her what would happen if I didn't get game time and she said that while it would be important, the fact I was in that environment would mean that she would know that I was getting pushed. She pretty much told me what I needed to do, but obviously the decision was still mine.

Vic had said that he wanted me to come down to Arsenal. He wanted me to see what they do and meet the manager. He told me that they wanted me there and that they could develop me, whether that was as a right-back, centre-back or central midfielder. He guaranteed that they would improve me as a player. You just get a moment where you're just like, Fuck it, I'm doing it. I'd finished at uni and it felt like the right time in my career, where I could just be a bit selfish. No regrets, right? I knew I could always go back north if I wanted to.

The best offer had actually come from Chelsea. Arsenal was £125 a game but then there was the chance of Champions League football, which would boost it a bit. They also said they would be able to help sort an apartment for me, which was huge, because obviously £125 a game isn't going to get you much. Carly Telford was going to Chelsea and so she moved in with me, which helped keep the rent down. We lived on Colney High Street, which was literally a two-minute walk from the Arsenal training ground.

Arsenal were great at doing everything they could. I ended up getting a £3,000 ambassador contract through the Women's Super League, which went towards bills, and I coached kids for a few days here and there at Arsenal's soccer schools. I also coached sports in primary schools just to make sure I had enough to get by. Central contracts had also been introduced for England players and so I got £16,000 a year from that, but obviously it was a struggle. You got taxed and most of the rest went on fuel and food.

The central contract thing was a big deal. They came in on the back of the 2009 Euros, after I had done my knee in. We were starting to become one of the best teams in the world and something had to change: people couldn't juggle full-time jobs and training as professional athletes. The introduction of central contracts was meant to allow people to still continue with work, but you could go part-time and limit it to sixteen hours a week. The £16,000 was meant to free you up so you could actually focus more on your training. Faye White was a massive part of that. She was the captain at the time, and she really drove those discussions. Obviously, I was a young player, so whatever Faye did, I was going to follow that. My understanding wasn't that great at the time, but to be able to get sixteen grand a year was unbelievable. I was still a student at the time, so I was absolutely buzzing. It meant I wouldn't have to get a job, so I could concentrate on my uni work and my training. I was already training full time so it didn't really affect me that much. But for other girls, it was a massive boost for them and for the game, because it allowed people to focus more on their football.

Hope picked the twenty-five to thirty players that she felt were going to go into the senior squad. Those who were selected were given a training programme with a plan for every month. The aim was to give us the best chance of winning things, because people were able to get a lot fitter and be a lot stronger. It meant that the FA started to take us seriously and was probably the best thing that could happen to us as female footballers. Now people were actually thinking we could do something really special. The people in power were looking at the situation and what it would take for us to be able to reach finals and compete with the likes of Germany and the USA.

I still had to supplement my salary, though, and the coaching gig was a struggle. Sometimes it was football but sometimes it was gymnastics. I didn't have a clue. In one session I thought I'd lost two of the kids, but it turned out they'd just gone to the loo. It was all a long way from where the game is now, but it was a case of needs must. I'm glad I did it because I think it does show you that there is a life outside football.

Sunderland was my first team and will always be my first team but pulling on that famous red Arsenal jersey with the white sleeves just felt right. And it wasn't only because I was surrounded by England teammates. There was Jayne Ludlow, who was Wales captain and an Arsenal legend. Unbelievable player. You had Scottish players like Julie Fleeting. And young players like Kim Little and Jennifer Beattie. They were getting game time even though they were so young, so I could see myself fitting in.

There was also an old friend. When we were leaving Leeds, me and Ellen White were talking about where we were going to go. She was adamant that she was going to go to Arsenal and it just kind of made sense.

Ellen is one of my best friends in football and we'd already shared a lot of experiences together so I was delighted we'd still be at the same club.

The first time we met was in an Under 19 game and I just remember – and she'll kill me for saying this – she had the biggest shin pads I've ever seen in my life. They were like cricket pads! I just remember thinking, Who is this girl? And she had a posh accent compared to me. She's from Aylesbury. She's so intelligent, her family are amazing, but then she was just a totally different person on the pitch. She gave absolutely everything in training and for me – I think that's why we got on so well. We always wanted the best for each other, and we pushed each other every single day in training. We were roomies and we were relaxed in each other's company. We could have a laugh and take the piss, but knew we didn't have to speak all the time and we knew when we just needed to chill. We were like peas in a pod, and I was thrilled when she said she was coming to Arsenal, not just because she was my best friend but because of what she brought as a player. Her finishing was incredible but her ability to press players was off the charts. Sometimes I'd be against her in training and I'd beg her to stop running. Her work rate was incredible.

I knew Vic Akers, and I knew he rated me as a player. I knew that he'd wanted to sign me since I was sixteen or seventeen, and for him to keep coming back meant something. I felt as though I needed to trust my instinct. I wanted to be there.

And it was exciting, but daunting at the same time. I had obviously lived away from home at uni, but I never had my own place. I was in digs at Loughborough, whereas now I had to find my own apartment. In London! Arsenal were amazing at that to be honest. They helped me settle quite quickly and subsidised the rent.

I will always remember the first day, when we went to the Emirates, the main stadium, for our photo shoot. That was a big deal. At the time it was one of the best grounds in the country and we had our picture taken with the men's team, which sounds silly now but it was huge at the time. No other club really did that. They never seemed to integrate the men's and women's teams. And my first ever picture was with Samir Nasri, the French international. We used to get paired up with a player and I was assigned Nasri. I was taller than him and I don't think he was too happy about that. He might have been thinking, Fuck off, I can't be arsed with this, but it was Arsenal and they wanted to do things properly.

That day was crazy because it was the day I signed. I got a flight down to London and went straight from the hotel to the Emirates for the photo shoot. I remember sitting on the plane, it was only forty minutes from Newcastle to London City, and thinking, Arsenal have paid for this. That was a big change because at Sunderland and Leeds it was always down to us to sort our transport.

I knew Laura Harvey, the coach, was good. She'd been there for a few years and they'd won things, and for me, my ambition was to win trophies. And I thought that the only way I could be sure I was going to win trophies was by going to Arsenal.

There were still areas that needed a lot of improvement. Nutrition, for example. We'd just have normal teas (I'm northern so it's tea, and not dinner). Me and Carly would just have things like baked potato and beans. Money was tight so we couldn't really go massive on protein. I didn't have a boot deal either – that didn't come until we went to the Olympics in 2012. If we needed anything, any boots, Vic would try and sort something. Because the club was sponsored by Nike, you might get the odd pair of boots here and there, but you'd probably be waiting a while until you got them. We were still buying our own. Don't get me wrong, Vic was great and would try and sort the girls out as much as he possibly could. He was amazing in that sense. He was resourceful and would try all different avenues at the club.

London was something else. I mean, I hated going into the city – I've got to be honest. It was too busy for me. I know London as a city is beautiful, but the fact is it's so busy and the people, they just weren't as friendly as people up north. I know lots of people say it, but you really notice it when you live there. Things like people holding doors open for you don't happen as much, and I noticed that people bump into you and don't even say sorry. It's just weird.

The hustle and bustle was not for me. I'm definitely not a city girl, that's for certain. I like to go out, and Cobham, had I gone to Chelsea, would have been perfect in the sense that it would be really easy to get into London. But at Colney we were close enough to be able to pop in. If we wanted to go for a walk there were places around there where we could escape a little bit. I did settle, but If I am being honest, it never really ever felt like home.

I also felt that I didn't have people that I loved around me and I found that difficult. Even when I was at Loughborough, I could always be home within a few hours, whereas it just wasn't as easy as that now. If I had a day off, I couldn't just nip up the road from London and go and see my family and friends. I missed having that little bit of protection. I think that hits hard, especially when you come from such a close-knit family. All my friends were scattered across the country by this stage, and it was quite hard.

I also think it's difficult when you're living with other teammates. There are times when you need your own space, an escape from football. I didn't have that, even if the girls I lived with during my time at Arsenal were amazing.

That said, Carly was brilliant. She's so funny. She made it very easy for me. Even though we were at different clubs, it was so natural. It might even have helped, because we could talk about work openly. Sometimes it was great to just know that there was someone there and we could kind of find our way together. We had already known each other from driving to Leeds together and had a great relationship. That first year still makes me smile. Even stupid little stuff we did, like sunbathing in our yard that was about two feet by two feet, pretending we were abroad but really wishing we had a proper garden!

The next year, we decided that we wanted to have a bigger house but obviously we couldn't afford that on our own, so we ended up living with Ellen White and Jordan Nobbs. The four of us were in a family house and London started to feel a little bit more like home.

But, oh my God, we were so different in terms of personalities. I think the one thing we had in common was that none of us was the tidiest. There'd be so many dishes, because we were always the entertainers and would have all the other girls over.

My mam used to go mad. She'd say that whenever she came round the place stank and there'd be dirty boots everywhere. At Arsenal, on the day you signed you got given a black bin liner full of kit. I can still remember it now. It was three lots of training kit, your home and away league kit and your home and away Champions League kit. We had to wash it ourselves and so whenever you came into the house there'd be shirts with Emirates, the club sponsor, on them all over the place. All you would see was Arsenal gear. On the washing line, on the radiators, everywhere.

I sometimes had to get my grandma to scrub my shorts because they were white and I just couldn't get the mud out. We'd synchronise our wash days so we didn't ruin anything. We'd have a home wash day and an away wash day, or a training wash day.

It's so embarrassing when I think about it now, but we were all absolutely buzzing that we had training kit, as we'd never had it before. It caused quite a few headaches, though. Because the responsibility was ours, we would be travelling to Kazakhstan for a Champions League game and we'd have to go through a checklist before we left the house. Have you got your training kit? Have you got your home kit? Have you got your away kit? It's crazy to think that as the biggest football club in the country we were trusted with that, but it is just how it was.

Aside from football, I didn't really have time for relationships, and I don't think living in London helped either. I wasn't that confident about going out and meeting boys and you didn't really have a network. It was just football and nothing else. To be honest, I was OK with that. I felt like I needed to take the next step in my career, and I didn't really need distractions. I was in my own little world. And yeah, the fact that you haven't got your own place doesn't help!

Ellen had met the man who is now her husband, Callum, when we were at uni. At Loughborough I was in a relationship with someone at home but that ended before I moved to Arsenal. I just wanted to make sure that I gave everything to this experience and, not in a boring way, kind of commit to it. A lot of the girls were in the same position. There were quite a few of us around the same age who were single and we had fun. We would just do what we wanted to do. I was quite enjoying being by myself and focusing on my football, to be honest.

Things really stepped up a gear at Arsenal. I think just

even wearing that badge on your chest and the feeling that you got when you wore the shirt – you're with those girls who had all achieved so much and who were hungry for more, and it increases your focus. Lots of people talk about pressure and how difficult it can be to deal with, but I take a different view. For me, that's when I start to enjoy it. I thrive on that pressure of expecting to win no matter what.

When we went to a final or we had a big game I would look around the changing room and think, We've got the best players in the world here. We've got players that have won multiple FA Cups, multiple league titles, and represented their countries. Who else would you want to go out and play alongside? It might sound like arrogance, but it wasn't, it was more a confidence. It was a confidence that we had everything we needed in this team. A confidence that we could thrive in adversity. A confidence that, whatever we had to face, we had the tools to get the job done. It was a feeling I had never had before and I loved it. I think I needed that experience, to get a feeling for that mentality.

I had never had that previously in my career, and that is absolutely no disrespect to Sunderland or to Leeds. But we were always the underdog at those clubs. We were never expected to win. The achievement was getting to the big occasions, not winning them. At Sunderland we were delighted just to get to the top division. At Leeds it was the same when we got to the FA Cup Final. We lost it 4–1 – to Arsenal – but that didn't take away from the achievement.

It was different now. There was a consistency with everything. The way that people arrived ready for training, the way that they applied themselves in the sessions, the things that we did in training. It was very structured, so we knew what we were doing and why we were doing it, which has always been a big thing for me. But it didn't make it any less exciting and the players we had there – honestly, I can't describe how good it was. People who don't really know me would probably think I'm quite confident on the pitch and in what I do. But back then I was a little bit insecure in myself and in what I brought because I'd had so much go on in my life in terms of ups and downs and setbacks.

When I was at Sunderland, I was probably the big dog, and it could feel like some people were just trying to knock you down as much as they possibly could. I know I'm guilty of thinking too much about what other people think about me.

Whereas at Arsenal it felt that the squad was focused and confident in what they were doing. They blocked out the noise. They got that confidence by training well, by bringing their best versions of themselves every single day, and by helping and driving the standard of the whole team.

Being able to observe individuals and the way they went about their business as a collective made it clear to me that I had made the right move. That's not to say it was all easy. I didn't play every game. I was in and out the team, and

I had known that was going to be the case, but it was the risk I needed to take to push myself as a player.

I also knew that when I got my chance, I needed to embrace the pressure to keep my shirt and to try and stay in the team. Even the final match of the season, when we had to win against Liverpool away, I was absolutely devastated not to start the game because it was such an important one. Eventually I got on with twenty minutes to go and was on the pitch when the whistle went and we were champions.

My dad, my grandma and my little cousin Aaron had come to that game because I think we all knew that we had a massive chance of winning the league.

These days, the trophy celebrations you see are really big deals, but for that one there was just a board with the name of the league on it. You just got handed the trophy and you all got your medals. And that was it. No fireworks or whatever else. No champagne. Me and Ellen were absolutely buzzing because it was our first trophy, but the other girls were just like, 'Yeah, just another one in the cabinet.' For me it was the first one, not just another one! In the back of my head I needed to justify why I moved to Arsenal. To win trophies. That was the reason I moved to the club. As soon as you lift that trophy and get all your pictures done and you see your family you get that sense of achievement, of vindication.

Nobody seemed to make a big deal of it, though. We literally just got on the bus straight back down to London.

A few of us went to a pub around the corner, but nothing major. If that was Leeds there would have been a riot!

At Arsenal, though, it just felt like the expected thing. People were set in what they did individually, and because they knew that they had the best players celebrating success wasn't such a big deal. That's where I'm different, and I think if I went into management I would make sure that my players celebrated every achievement. It's a big thing and you never know where the next win is going to come from.

We also got to the FA Cup Final and played Bristol at the Ricoh Arena in Coventry. My main memory from that is of how chilled everyone was before the game.

And I was sitting there wondering if I should feel relaxed or nervous. That was a weird one for me because I have never had that situation or emotion before. But from the first whistle, people were just playing with so much freedom, like it was the most normal thing in the world. That instantly gave me confidence, and when you win that first trophy it feels like a huge moment in your career. That FA Cup was the first proper trophy I ever got my hands on. And it was such a big occasion. It was on television, it was in front of all my family, and in front of a big crowd of about fourteen thousand. To get that one over the line was huge. It kind of underlined that I'd made the right decision in moving to Arsenal. I was like, '*This* is why I moved.' We were expected to win, which was a new feeling. That's not to say that Bristol didn't give us a tough game. They had been on an amazing run and were managed by a guy called Mark Sampson. His teams were always well drilled, well organised and well coached. But our players stepped up. Julie Fleeting was a standout for me. She was ultra-professional. She never used to train with us, she would just fly down from Scotland on the morning of a game and then go out and bag a hat trick. She had her life up there with her husband, and she worked as a teacher. But the club made allowances because she was so good. She was ridiculous, and she scored against Bristol. I loved the feeling of winning, of achieving, and it made me hungry for more.

Everyone demanded high standards. Jayne Ludlow, honestly, was one of the best box-to-box midfielders I have ever seen. The way she got up and down the pitch. Just an absolute engine and she'd love a header too. She had this ability to just take the game by the scruff of the neck. She was captain for a reason: she was the one that drove the team forward and you could see that. She was the one who set the standards, but she wasn't the only one. Rachel Yankey made sure she had a word with me on my first day, which was massive for me.

We had spoken about where I was going to play before I joined Arsenal and as things played out, I got the number two because they saw me as a right-back. In my first season I was predominantly there.

It was a year of new experiences. My first Champions

League trip was to Serbia against a team called ZFK Masinac. It was the first time I had played in a really hostile environment. So hostile. There was also a lot of racism towards our black players, which was horrendous. Monkey chants every time Rachel, say, or Dan Carter touched the ball. They were getting booed simply because of the colour of their skin. I struggled to take it all in. I remember thinking, Is this what Champions League football is about? Is this what people actually think?

We hadn't been warned about it before the game, so I don't know if the others had experienced it before and kind of expected it. Maybe they had blocked it out or were prepared for it, but I wasn't and it shocked me. It was difficult to concentrate on the game because I was worried about my teammates and how it was impacting them.

There were positives from being in the competition. It went up another level in terms of the quality of the players. It was another eye-opener for me. It felt like you were playing international football with your club team. The standard was through the roof, and it was a valuable learning experience about the standard I needed to be at.

And to hear the Champions League anthem – the women's one is different from the one they play at men's games – and to see that badge on your arm. I don't know. It's difficult to explain how that makes you feel.

In my early experiences of the Champions League I also witnessed one of the biggest tantrums I had ever seen. After we'd played in Serbia, we went to Spain to play against Rayo Vallecano. Again, it was a hostile atmosphere.

We didn't start great, but Jayne was probably at fault for their two goals. At half-time she came into the changing room. And obviously, I was young and not really at the point where I would say what I really think because there were older, more experienced players saying that. Rachel, Ciara Grant, Emma Byrne – they would always have a voice and say it in different ways, but Jayne just came in absolutely screaming. She was fuming. Water bottles went flying everywhere. The tactics board was thrown into the showers. I was sitting with my mates, with Ellen and Jordan, all hoping that she wasn't going to come for us. We were trying to think whether we'd done anything wrong she could have a go at us for. She was blaming everybody else for those two goals! And I was thinking, I don't think it was anybody else's fault – you were the one who gave the ball away! But obviously I wasn't going to come out and say that. Those moments, pure raw emotion – you don't tend to get them in football any more, and I think that's a shame. People actually being able to show how much they care, regardless of whether they're at fault. I just love the fact that Jayne wore her heart on her sleeve and gave absolutely everything for the football club, and that kind of epitomised her as a character. She was definitely someone I learned a lot from in terms of the competitive edge and the will to win. I often used to think about what she would do in a situation, even after I left Arsenal.

I've still got those Champions League shirts at home. I try to keep as many as I possibly can, because when I have kids one day I think they would want to see them and to know that their mam played in the Champions League and competed against the best players in Europe.

It was all pretty intense, mind. The fact that you travel overseas and play the next day. You often didn't even get a chance to train. Literally you either get there the night before or even the morning of the game and then you go out and play. That was a new experience for me, too.

LIFE CHANGER

The 2011 World Cup fell in the middle of that season and, given what had happened with injuries previously, I was pretty apprehensive in the run-up to it. I wasn't pulling out of challenges or anything like that, but I did try to slow myself down a little bit. I did everything properly, but I made sure that I wasn't trying to do everything at a hundred miles an hour, which is the type of person I usually am. I told myself to take it easy, make sure I did my training properly, get looked after, make sure I saw the physio if I needed to.

This time, thank God, there was no last-minute injury in the gym or bad tackle. The feeling when I made the squad was almost one of relief. I was just so glad to be there. I didn't really care about my position or how much I was going to play. The main thing was being on the plane to Germany. I knew I was going as a back-up right-back, but I had played a bit in midfield for Arsenal and had done well so I knew I'd be useful as I was versatile. At the time Alex Scott was still by far the best right-back, and rightly so with all her experience.

In the build-up I think Alex pulled a quad. We had a few friendly matches, in which I thought I'd done OK, and Alex was touch and go. But she was always going to be first choice if she could get fit and that's what ended up happening.

We won the group and finished above Japan, who we beat 2–0 in the final game. It was a breakthrough tournament for Ellen and I was really proud of her.

I hadn't managed to get any playing time, but then in the quarter-final against France I was thrown on in extra time. I wasn't expecting it, and it was pretty scary. I just wanted to make sure I didn't do anything wrong.

The game finished 1–1 and we ended up losing on penalties, which was tough to take. Back then, I wouldn't say we practised taking them so much. The likes of Fara Williams, who was the designated penalty-taker, or Kelly Smith, placed a lot of emphasis on it. They knew that if we had a penalty, chances were that they would be taking it. But the rest of us didn't practise that much. You could say that was a mistake, but it just wasn't a thing – which is mad, because there was always going to be the possibility in the knockout stages that your whole tournament would come down to them.

I remember standing on halfway with the girls and I was

honestly really confident because we had played so well in the game. Jill Scott had had an unbelievable tournament and was great again, but France were a very, very good side with a lot of experience and I guess it just wasn't meant to be. We actually went 1–0 up but then Claire Rafferty missed, and when Faye White hit the bar, that was that. I was next up, and I was preparing myself for it. I didn't think for a second it would be over by then. I was thinking about where I was going to put it, what I was going to do. I always tended to put my penalties to one side and this would have been no different. My thought is always that, with my technique, if I get a clean strike it's going in. Sitting here now, thinking about how we didn't practise, it sounds absolutely crazy.

Faye had been a great captain, and it was devastating for her. I felt sick. There was a lot of talk that this would be her final tournament – which turned out to be right – and she didn't need all the France players running past her, celebrating in her face. At the time I thought they were out of order. With certain nations, there's a bit more of an intense rivalry and I didn't like that. Looking back, I'd say it was probably just joy for them, that they'd got through. I was absolutely gutted for Faye. She had been with me since I made my debut. I didn't want her to be left alone at that moment, so I sprinted across as quickly as I could to give her a hug. I knew that she would have done that for me if the roles were reversed.

The loss strengthened my desire to win something with England, but even though we were knocked out it would be wrong to say I didn't enjoy my first tournament.

Once you're in that environment, it's not just about the games it's also about the experience. I love travelling to different places, and I know it sounds stupid, but the free stuff that you get, the hotels you see – it's all part of it. Even the little things, like a free washbag. I think I came home with twice as much as I went with, given all the freebies you get!

To go as a young player, to experience that, was amazing. I tried to take pictures of absolutely everything. And the tournament felt like a big deal in Germany itself. The fact that when you go into different cities there are posters on the lamp posts, flags everywhere. And that feeling of travelling the country on the England team bus was crazy.

We also got the sense that our sport was taking off at home, although you're obviously detached from that. I knew that we were on television, but back then social media hadn't really taken off like it has now. There was Twitter, but no Instagram. So we were quite cut off from everybody. I also didn't have to do too many interviews because it was predominantly the girls who started.

The next major tournament was the 2012 Olympics, which was being held in London. In football, Team GB wasn't really a thing, but it just felt huge. It was going to be the best players from Britain playing against the best players in the world. So what wasn't there to be excited about? I think the women's game has a different approach to the Olympics from the men's, and that comes from the Americans, who take it so seriously.

The USA have always been the benchmark. You want to emulate them or surpass them. Their players always spoke about the importance of winning a gold medal, and the likes of Mia Hamm and Carli Lloyd were global superstars. We knew that Hope was going to be manager because the FA primarily funded the build-up, and as soon as I heard that there would be a team, I wanted to be part of it.

A lot of England players were in the squad, and from the start, from the opening ceremony with the Queen involved, it was amazing. I had been looking forward to it and I was determined to embrace it, but I never, ever expected it to be as good as it was. If people ask me now what my favourite tournament was, I would probably have to say that one. And it wasn't just because of the football; it was the whole package. Being in that environment, being involved with different athletes and getting to know how they work, being in the Olympic Village – it's just a different world. I also got my first pair of proper free boots. Team GB were sponsored by Adidas, and they gave us three pairs!

We weren't in the Olympic Village to start with. We had a training camp up at Rockcliffe Hall near Middlesbrough. We were there with the men's team, with the likes of

Ryan Giggs and Craig Bellamy. It was an eye-opener to be around elite men's players and to get a view of how they prepared. And they were great with us.

I didn't really speak to Craig Bellamy that much but the likes of Giggs, Micah Richards and Aaron Ramsey were great. We used to play cards with them downstairs in the hotel because we had nothing else to do.

We made the trip to London for one night, to go to the Olympic Village to see what it was like. But as soon as we were back, we were like, OK, we've got four days until our first game, which was at the Millennium Stadium in Cardiff. To start in the Olympic Games was unbelievable, and that first game against New Zealand was quite a tough opener. It was really hot and there were probably over twenty-five thousand fans there. All my family had travelled down, and it was a fairly even first half.

We got a free kick, pretty central, about twenty-five yards out, midway through the second half, and I wanted to take it. I used to practise them a lot and the day before we'd been practising from different positions. I had a chat with Kelly Smith, who normally takes them, and she asked me if I wanted it. We'd noticed the keeper was leaving a big gap to her right and I thought that if I hit it well, that's where it would go. So Kelly ran over the ball to distract them, and I hit it. As soon as it left my boot, I knew it was in. I'd put a bit of curl on it and I just knew that from where the keeper was standing, she had no chance of getting there.

It hit the back of the net and I just ran off like an idiot. I didn't really think about it being the first ever goal for a women's Team GB, I was just delighted we were winning, because we'd missed a load of chances.

We were back to the same stadium for the next game, against Cameroon, and this one was a bit easier. We won 3–0 and I scored again, smashing one into the bottom corner, although earlier on Jill had scored what was probably the goal of the tournament!

We moved down to the Olympic Village before the final group game, which was against Brazil. The village was interesting. We were in dorms, so about six of us sharing three rooms with a kitchen, and obviously I was with Ellen. I'm not sure how the men's team got on because they had to do the same thing!

When it's time to eat you go to this massive dining room, and I was amazed at what was on offer. There was hardly anything nutritious – there was a McDonald's in there. So if you really wanted to get a McDonald's you could get a McDonald's. Everything was free, all the stuff from the sponsors was there: Coca-Cola, Powerade, anything you wanted. And it was always open, so if you wanted to go at three in the morning you could. You could tell when athletes had finished competing, because the queue for McDonald's got a bit longer. Normally after you'd finished a game you would go back and rest, but because you're in a village, everybody's out everywhere, so you tend to go out.

And we had our accreditation so we could go and watch other events, which was really cool. There was also booze, but we stayed away from that while we were competing.

For me, Brazil was massive. I'd never played at Wembley before and I couldn't wait. To go to the home of football, where there have been so many amazing moments throughout history, was unbelievable.

We went out to warm up and I had goosebumps. There were seventy thousand people there. I'd never seen anything like it. Everybody was so excited to see us. We had won the two games prior and were on a roll, and now we were playing against Brazil, a country everybody loves. Playing against Brazil, because of what they have done historically, the flair that they have, was unreal. In their team they had Marta, who's an absolute legend, maybe the greatest of all time. We knew it was going to be a tough game and we wanted to start on the front foot.

As soon as it kicked off, we got a corner. We were good on corners, and I always thought we had a chance of scoring. We were quite physical in the sense that we were tall and we had good delivery: the likes of Kaz Carney and Kim Little could put good balls in.

Anyway, the ball gets cleared out and I'm thinking I should really be going back to my position, but I just stayed there because it was Kaz on the ball. I was meant to be at the back post, but I thought if I can get to the near post and she sees me, there's some space there. Kaz spots me and my first touch takes me past the keeper but it's a tight angle. I hit it and the next thing I can remember was the noise of the crowd. I was thinking, How the fuck have I managed to get that in there? I ran off like an idiot again and did a knee slide, but I was also thinking that there were still eighty-eight minutes to play and I knew we would have to defend a lot.

You don't think it at the time, because you're twenty-four and you're in the middle of a game, but when I look back on my career, that is one of the moments that made it all worthwhile. All that practising, all that kicking the ball against the pole in the backyard. You realise how many people love you and how many people have supported you, and in a moment like that you know that it was all worth it.

We played Canada at Coventry in the quarter-final, and we struggled with their star player, Christine Sinclair. We did a lot of analysis before every game and Hope was very good with our tactical game plans, but I always felt that if we didn't go a goal ahead and the other team did, what was our plan B? And Sinclair was one of the best strikers I've ever played against. She can pop in into midfield, get on the ball, and as a centre-half or a defender it's hard to pick someone up like that. We were missing Kelly Smith as well, as she got injured in the Brazil game. She was one of our best players and really drove the team forward. Canada had obviously done their homework on us, and I didn't play my greatest game, but we just didn't really have an answer to their goals. It was still a positive experience for us, because it was the first time we'd been involved in a tournament where you play in huge games and then only have a few days to pick yourself up and go again.

Despite us going out, it did feel like a big moment for women's football. We stayed mostly at the Marriott in the centre of Cardiff, and there were loads of paper shops on the main street, where I would see my face on the back pages, which was surreal. I'd get messages from friends saying 'Oh my God, Steph, you're in the *Mirror*, you're in the *Mail*.' I think the *Mail* sent a reporter to my family's house, which was bizarre. It gripped the nation and we saw a spike in attendances when the domestic season re-started after the Games.

To be fair, the media were amazing. They really wanted to push the Olympics, and it was great for the journalists who covered women's football, because they had been with us when it wasn't as big and it was good for them to come on the journey with us. I wasn't media trained, I'd hardly spoken to the press and I didn't have an agent, so there was no protection for me in that sense, but I just felt like we had to get out there and speak because we wanted to do something for women's football.

It really hit me after the game against Brazil. Me and Ellen went back to our room and I swear to God we probably had about half an hour's sleep the whole night. I went from two hundred followers on Twitter to about twenty-five thousand overnight. I was like, 'Ellen, what's happening?' She loved it. She was telling me that Kelly Holmes had tweeted me, which was massive because she had come in to give us a talk before the Olympics started on what it all meant. And then Sunderland started following me, which was crazy. My phone was lighting up and it carried on like that all night.

That tournament changed my life. I started getting recognised. Our village is a small one, and if I went to the shop then my grandma would know exactly what time I went there and what I'd bought. People would come up to me and say, 'You're that girl who scored three goals, aren't you?' I'd ask them if they knew my name, which they did. It was mad. I'd be chilling in a pub with my teammates from Arsenal and people would come over. I found the whole thing crazy.

There was a bit of creepy stuff. Like random, weird messages on social media. Although it wasn't until I moved to City that it got pretty bad. You'd get message requests and people just randomly asking for pictures of your feet and stuff. Who wants to see my feet?! I've probably got one big toenail, and that's about it! So we have a laugh now if I get something like that.

I have to admit it was difficult going back to Arsenal after the Games. It's always hard to get yourself going again after a major tournament, because you've been on such a massive high or a massive low. The Arsenal manager told us they needed us back in a week and we were like, 'Fucking hell – we've just been away for seven weeks.' It was difficult to get motivated, but we got down to business and managed to win the league again.

'THAT'S ALL YOU GET?'

Not long after the Olympics, *Match of the Day* wanted to do an interview with me, which felt like a big deal because if you're English and you like football you will have watched *Match of the Day* at some point.

The way that it used to work was that if anybody from the media wanted to do anything with you they would go through the club. Then it would come to the players. Faye White was working at Arsenal by then, and she got an email request for me to go up to Salford, to film the interview. She said the BBC would pay for my train up to Manchester and I'd get £100 for two hours' work.

I was happy to do it as long as it wasn't on a training day, and I was actually a bit excited by it. Faye said she thought I might get quite a few requests over the next few months because of how the Olympics had gone. She was smart, Faye, and mentioned that it might be worth trying to get someone to help look after me. I'd never really thought about it, because at the time, not many people in the women's game had agents. My dad sorted out my deal with Arsenal, but when I say that I am probably overplaying it. It wasn't like there was much conversation or haggling involved.

At the time of the interview request I had my £16,000 from my central contract from England and I was on about £3–4,000 a year from Arsenal, plus bonuses. I think in total, if we had a good year, I'd get £6,000 from the club, with an extra £3,000 for being an ambassador and doing the coaching.

Anyway, Faye said she would speak to a woman called Marie, Marie-Christine Bouchier, who worked for the Professional Footballers' Association and might be able to help out.

I was a bit scared, if I'm being honest, about what Faye said about the attention and requests. I couldn't really figure out why anyone would want to speak to me. It just didn't make any sense.

When I think about it, now that I am older, I recognise why certain people get picked for certain things and I understand the reason why, but at the time I was just like, there's so many other people that you could speak to.

So I went up to Salford. Marie was busy, so she sent one of her colleagues from the PFA, a bloke called Matthew Buck, and we met in a Costa Coffee just next to MediaCity. He asked me how much I was getting for the interview, and he nearly fell off his chair when I told him. He didn't even know me, but he was raging on my behalf. He was the agent for James Milner, who was playing for the England men's team at the time, so he knew what other people were getting offered. He said that we'd do this interview for now, but if I was happy, he could look after me as my agent. He also said that we would need to have a conversation, as we could not accept that kind of fee in future. For me, that was quite a big moment, where I began to think that things needed to change.

Matt and I have had such a good relationship from that day in Costa until now. He's been pivotal to my whole career. There can be a bit of a stigma about agents and how they are, like shady characters and stuff, but Matt's more of a friend than an agent, not just for me but for Stephen, my husband, as well. He supports us, even sometimes just being that person you can speak to when you're a bit fuming after training – instead of ranting at Stephen, I'm ranting at him, just to get it off my chest. All the decisions that I've made, I would never have been able to do it without Matt.

And when you think about the people who have changed women's football, he is probably one of the most important, especially with negotiating England contracts and commercial deals. He was the one that really pushed and really stood up for us.

Matt is also not the type to take credit for it. He'll probably hate that he's mentioned in this book, to be honest.

But I think that's what makes a good agent: the fact that it's never about them, it's about everybody else and what they can do, while they go quietly about their business. Matt is very, very good at what he does and I'm very lucky to have him as my agent. I probably have Faye to thank for that.

In 2012, the Arsenal contracts were not really proper contracts compared to what we have now. We would only ever sign for a year, so in pre-season, you'd be training and basically one day was contracts day at the club. One by one we would get called in to Vic's office and there would be a contract in front of him on the desk. You'd be sweating and knackered and you wouldn't even look at it. There was no conversation, not one bit of negotiation. It was just, 'We can offer you this – sign here.' You'd sign it and then you would go back out on the pitch. Honestly.

When I met Matt, he also asked me what my club contract looked like. I went through it and he just kept on shaking his head as if to say, 'That's all you get?' I had to tell him I wasn't lying. That's all I play for. He couldn't believe it. He kept asking me if my contract was really only worth up to £7,000. I still remember him saying, 'This stops now.' I didn't really know what he meant. He asked me how it worked, so I went through it. How we would all be training, how we would get called into the office and how we would sign the piece of paper that was put in front of us. Matt asked me if I was joking. I think he thought I was taking the mickey. He told me he couldn't believe it.

That I'd been playing for two years for what they had been paying. But I had come from nothing, so for me, that contract was everything. And, more importantly, I was happy. I was playing football with some of the best players in the world and in the country. I was winning trophies. And he was like, 'Yeah, but Steph, you're at the club that's the best in the country.' He told me we needed to push, and we needed to raise the standard for everybody.

He told me that the next time I was offered a new contract, I was forbidden from signing it. He told me to go in and tell Vic that I couldn't sign anything until my agent had looked it over. My God, I felt sick when he said that. I'd seen the way Vic was, I knew that he was an unbelievable person, and had done so much for women's football. As a person and for me and my career, he was amazing. So I trusted him with absolutely everything and honestly didn't know if I would be able to do it, to say no, I'm not signing. As you know by now, I want to please people all the time and this just wasn't me, but I knew Matt was right and that I'd have to do it. It didn't stop me from absolutely shitting myself the night before, though.

But I did it. I said I wouldn't sign and that I needed Matt to take a look at the contract first. I think I was the only player with an agent. Everyone else's dads did it for them, like mine had for me. I told them that Matt would kill me if I signed it. I talked it through with Ellen and she told me I had to do what I had to do. I was petrified. I thought they

95

might withdraw the contract entirely, but Ellen said there was no chance they would do that. I had so many things running through my head. Given where I had come from, playing for Sunderland and Leeds, I just thought I was so lucky to play at Arsenal. But Matt had made me realise that things had to change, that we had a value and we had to be paid properly for what we did for the club. That wasn't just me, but everybody else as well. So having that conversation with Vic was pretty tough.

I was bracing myself, and Vic asked me to come into his office. It was literally a room to the side of the building where we were training. As was the norm, he asked me to sign the contract. I steeled myself and forced myself to ask him if he minded if I took it away. He asked me what for. I asked him if it was OK for my agent to look at it first. He seemed pretty surprised by that. He asked me again if I wanted to sign it, and when I said I needed to show it to my agent he just said 'OK' and walked out. God, it was so awkward. But for all the awkwardness and the feeling of dread and the fact I didn't get any sleep the night before, it did feel like I'd done the right thing. It felt like I was taking a stand not just for me but for everyone else as well.

I took the contract to Matt and he was convinced that we could up it. It was basically another £6,000. He managed to get an increase. It wasn't massive, but it was more about the principle. It felt like a big moment. A line in the sand.

After that, things started to change. In the third season,

the pushing a contract under your face during training situation didn't happen again – for me or for anybody else. It was more meeting-led, and you'd arrange a time and an appointment. More and more of us were getting agents. The whole process started to become a bit more professional and I felt like we'd played a big part in that. It was the best Costa I've ever bought, anyway!

LEAVING LONDON

I had my new contract for 2013 and the team had a new manager. Laura Harvey was offered a job in Seattle, and the women's league in America was really starting to pick up. I think she'd always wanted to go. Kim Little had played there for a long time. I think it was a job you just couldn't say no to and the chance to go to America was huge.

Shelley Kerr had come down from managing Scotland's Under 19s, and she told me I was going to be vice-captain. I was only twenty-five and I know it didn't go down well with a lot of the girls. Some of them thought I was too young and there were others who had been in the squad for a lot longer than me who hadn't had the privilege.

People started acting differently towards me. I wore the captain's armband a lot that season because Kelly Smith was injured for the majority of the time. I had no intention of even thinking about the captaincy, I was just happy to be able to keep my spot, to keep playing, to keep playing for England. And I never, ever dreamt in a million years that I'd be captain of Arsenal – it was as shocking to me as it was to anyone. But sometimes when a new manager comes in, they want to stamp their authority on the team. There were a lot of players that were getting a bit older as well, so I think it was kind of one for the future.

It's sad to say, but people started to avoid me a little bit. A lot of people were good with me, but there were some who you just knew were talking about you behind your back or talking about the situation. I don't think it was me, personally. I think it was more to do with the manager and the fact that she'd picked me. Of course, it's a big thing being captain of a club or being associated with the leadership group or whatever it might be. As a young player, my head was just in overdrive, to be honest. My old trait of wanting to be liked by everyone came to the fore again and I wanted people to know that I was still the same person regardless of whether I was captain, vice-captain or not. I did feel a bit of pressure. It was a difficult situation.

That said, I did see it as a natural progression. For me, the way that I've always played, I've always been quite vocal. From a young age my dad always taught me that you need to be able to speak, you need to be able to communicate. And playing the position that I do, I can see everything. I like to think that my understanding of the game is at a good level, and when we do have messages or tactics I can remember them and I can help people in certain scenarios. I knew it was a strength of mine in terms of being vocal on the pitch.

Regardless of how it went down with some of the others, being vice-captain of Arsenal is massive, especially when you think about all the people who have done it before you. Some absolute legends have held that role and it was a big moment for me. I was never going to say no. Why should I? I'd been there for two years. I was gaining experience all the time. I'd learned from a lot of people. I'd like to think that I'd give everything to the club, so it was another step on in my football career.

I can still remember Shelley telling everyone. It was a bit abrupt, a bit off the cuff, and I don't think that helped. She just literally came into a training session, told me and then announced it to the team straight away. She'd pulled me to one side and said that she wanted me to be vice-captain. I was like, *Me?!* I think I even asked her if she was sure, and whether she didn't think she should be offering it to someone else. She told me that she could see leadership skills in me and that she felt as though I could help the team. I was shocked and still trying to process it, but within two minutes she had told the whole team. I'd not even been able to tell my mam and dad!

It was a strange season. Kelly got injured in a Champions League game and I remember her coming over and sliding the armband on. I couldn't believe that I had been given the opportunity, that she was putting it on me. It was a very strange feeling. But it brought the best out of me, being captain. I always want to lead by example and try to be the best that I can be. You kind of get a little bit more energy by having the armband on and having a little bit more responsibility.

We finished second in the league that year which was a massive disappointment, but we won the FA Cup and the League Cup. The FA Cup is one of my favourite memories. We played Bristol at Doncaster, and I scored after two minutes. It's something you absolutely dream of. We won 3–0 – Nobbsy and Ellen got the other two goals – and when it was time to lift the trophy I wanted to make sure I did it with Kelly because she was the captain and an absolute hero, an unbelievable girl. For me, it wasn't really about the trophy, it was more about seeing how happy everyone else was – my teammates, my family.

I could see my family at the trophy lift and it's something I won't forget. I often think those moments are more for them than they are for us. They travel everywhere to see us, and you sacrifice so much, being away in London and being away from them. For us all to come together and know that that's all worthwhile, that's one of the biggest things. That was probably my best day at Arsenal. I always remember Yanks saying to me, 'Steph, it's more about the day than the actual game.' She told me to make sure I took it all in, soaked everything up. Even the journey up, the journey to Coventry, the journey to Doncaster, that's what you remember. You don't really remember that much of the games, but the pre-match nerves, the build-up to the national anthem, you just want to soak it all in. Ever since she said that, I always tell players that play in the final, Girls, no matter what, just embrace it all because you don't get these chances that often in football, you're lucky if you maybe get one or two finals.

To be told that really calmed me down. The pressure was on but because she was so used to it, she just knew how to act, and for her to say that was pretty cool. Yanks was really good at that sort of stuff.

I was still loving it at Arsenal. We were having a great time, the four of us in the house. And I loved our new manager. Shelley gave us so much trust and she was the first person that actually made me into a proper centre-half. Until then I had been playing all over. A bit in midfield, a bit at right-back, a bit at left-back – I didn't really have one position. Shelley had identified that I could be a centre-half, and she made things really simple in the training sessions. She had us in there, defending crosses, and really taught me to know my position, to be able to lead the line and that communication style and body position. I remember doing drills in the indoor dome and really enjoying the smaller details that I'd probably missed before.

At the time, there was a lot of talk about Manchester

City putting a bid in to join the WSL. So much talk. They were a huge deal because the club had been taken over by Sheikh Mansour, who had transformed the men's team – they had already won the Premier League. We were away at Liverpool when the story broke on Twitter, and one of the girls mentioned it in the dressing room.

I didn't say it out loud, but I just thought to myself that surely they were just going to go all in and buy loads of players. But I wasn't thinking that it would be me or anybody else. I just knew that they would have to do it properly and that they must have had a great bid to be able to get in, because otherwise why would they have taken Doncaster out the league, when they had so much history and so many amazing players? We then played Everton at Marine and word got around that some people from City were there. I was in midfield and I played pretty well. We won 2–1 and in the next few days Matt got a call from a guy called Gavin Makel, who was the general manager at City.

Gav asked if it was OK for them to speak to me about the prospect of going to play for them. Matt told them that I was really happy at Arsenal. But he asked me, and I told him I'd be lying if I said I didn't want to know what City had to say.

Throughout my career my stance has always been that I want to get all the information before making a decision rather than just making a decision without knowing what's actually happening or who said what.

Matt told me that we were going to have to be really careful because I was under contract, and clubs are not allowed to make an approach while that's the case. The reality is that everyone speaks to everyone. It happens all the time. We had to make sure that we did it around training and that it never impacted on my Arsenal time.

I think even then, even though I didn't know what it was going to be or how it would look, in the back of my mind I wanted to move closer to home, and Manchester was a lot closer. I felt like I'd done the London thing. I'd lived away from home. I was at the stage in my life where I wanted to buy my own house and there was no chance of me doing that in London because of how expensive it was.

I'd managed to save a little bit, but I was always wondering how much more I could save if I moved to the North-East or the North-West, and houses up there were so much more affordable. I could maybe buy somewhere in my old village at home.

So I was thinking more about life things. It would be wrong to say I was sick of living with the girls because I wasn't. We had some great times. But I was sick of not having a place of my own. You get to a point where you want your own thing. I wasn't seeing anybody and I had no ties to London, so I thought I'd go and see City.

It didn't take them long to make a big impression. It turned out they had an office in London, because obviously they would. Matt said we were going to meet Brian

Marwood. I had no clue who that was. He told me that it was Brian Marwood who had played for Arsenal and who was now one of the senior people at City. Matt said just to trust him on the negotiations: James Milner was playing for City at the time, so he already had a good relationship with these people. He told me that he knew how they worked, and he knew that they were going to do things properly. He said that whatever they promised me in the meeting, they would go through with it.

But I needed Matt to understand that things were going well for me. I was vice-captain at Arsenal and I was playing for England. I was playing with all these great players. But he just told me to listen to what City had to say and then we could make a call later on. He said I could always say no. So we went to this meeting with Brian Marwood. And honestly, you go into these plush offices and it's glitzy and it's got pictures of Man City everywhere.

So we get in and I'm nervous as hell because I've never really been presented to like this before. Matt told me just to listen and that we'd go away and assess what the plan is. I liked Brian straight away. He was from the North-East like me, and he was really humble. He told me straight up that they were new to this and that it was a project. He told me that success was not going to happen in one year. He was really straight with me. But he was also confident. He said success would happen, but it was going to be over a number of years and that they needed great people to be in at the start. He told me that he wanted me to be part of it, and that they wanted people that were going to trust them and really drive the club forward. He also showed us the plans for the City Football Academy, a huge training complex that they were building next to the Etihad Stadium. He told me that we would have our own part of the training room and that we would also have our own stadium, which was a massive thing. At Arsenal, we played at the Emirates a couple of times, but we were mostly playing our home games at Borehamwood, which was a non-league stadium.

He said the full-time professionals they were going to bring in would train during the day and then train again with the rest of the team at night. At first they wanted to give a chance to some of the local girls who weren't full-time, which I thought was fair enough.

I kept thinking that I would be going from Arsenal, where it was training four times a week, to training every day. At the time that's what I needed – to be on the ball every single day and to learn something new.

So we go away from this meeting and I'm thinking that while Arsenal are a fantastic club with a manager that's really trusted me and with great players, this is exciting. This is different. This is a project and a massive opportunity. The chance to be involved in something at the start and stay in the centre of it for a long time. I was also delighted that they wanted me. All those players out there, and they want me and a few others to start this thing off.

What had happened with the men's team was also a massive pull. A year earlier was the Aguero moment, when Sergio Aguero scored in injury time in what was probably the greatest finish to a Premier League season in history. I looked into that, about City's past and how it had been so long since they had won anything. And then the new owners came in and put all this investment not just into the club but into the city itself. There's been massive regeneration of the area next to the stadium. It's unreal.

Once I had that chat with Brian and Gav, I definitely wanted to find out more. The fact that they were building a whole new training facility was huge. As women, we would have our own changing room. We didn't get that at Arsenal. We literally just turned up in our training kit. We would get changed at home. When we got in from training, we'd all put our training kit in the wash and just hang it up. Everybody would do the same. We'd get changed at home and drive to the training ground. It was only five minutes from home, so I guess we were lucky, but when it's pissing it down and you're wet through when you get in the car afterwards, it wasn't pleasant.

But at the same time, that was a step up from where I had been before. So to now potentially go to City, where you would have your own changing room and you've got your own stadium, you're able to train full time and be close to home, began to sound like a no-brainer. We would even have people washing our kit! And not only that, we would have a team of people to help us. But it wasn't just about getting kit washed and stuff like that. I was striving for more professionalism. I was striving for us to be on a par with the lads, and to make the women's game the best it could be. Those little things matter; people might think they don't, but when you're in it they do. That respect that everybody has for you as a female and also as a footballer has to be there. The men have set that standard, and we are working to get up to it. Going away from that meeting I was a bit confused, to be honest, my head was all over the place.

I absolutely loved Arsenal and I loved how I was playing. I loved everything about it, but my gut was saying I needed a change. I agreed to another meeting, which this time was in Manchester. I went up to the Etihad, met Gav again and also met Nick Cushing, who was going to be the coach. We spoke about where I potentially could play and he obviously wanted me to play as number six, just in front of the back four, because that's where I predominantly played at Arsenal.

We were in one of the suites in the Etihad, overlooking the pitch. At the time, Mark Sampson had come in as England manager or was just coming in. Brent Hills was caretaker manager for England. And he wanted me to play as a centre half. So my mind was like, I need to come here and I need to be in one position. I need to be playing centre half and the way that City wanted me to play, I would have a lot of the ball. So I told them that I knew they wanted me to play six but I needed to make sure I was in the national team and I needed to learn how to play centre-half properly – and be coached on that every single day.

They agreed to that, which was a big, big factor in terms of me going. It was a non-negotiable. And then we went over to City Football Academy. It was just a building site. A massive building site. We went on with our hard hats and yellow jackets in the little digger things, and went round and imagined what it was going to be like.

They showed us where our changing room was going to be. They said, 'This will be your stadium. This is where you'll drive in.' You start to picture it, and you get excited.

We didn't speak about length of contract or how much money they were offering at that stage. But Matt after we came away from the meeting told me that we needed to start talking numbers and I gave him the green light to do that.

I didn't have a number in my head whatsoever. And it was getting closer and closer to the Arsenal season ending. I was going to be off for the whole of December because of the way that the league was set up. And Matt was telling me that City needed a decision. They were starting to build their team: Toni Duggan had already announced that she was going to be moving there, which was a big deal because she was a great striker.

I was still wondering about who else was going to go. I asked Matt if he knew, and he told me he thought Jill Scott was going. I thought about phoning her, but it was awkward because I knew she was really happy at Everton.

Maybe I would now, but back then, I didn't want to pry that much. The rumours were there, though, and once I was getting close to signing I actually messaged her asking her what she was doing. Typical Jill: she messaged me back, asking me what I was doing. It was pretty awkward. I replied, telling her I thought that sky blue would suit us. To be fair to City, they had kind of shown me the team that they wanted to bring in, but there were big question marks over some people, like Izzy Christiansen, for example.

Goalkeeper was a massive one for me. And it was no offence to the goalkeepers that were already at City, but I'd told them that if we were going to have any chance we would need a great goalkeeper. Especially in those first few years. I asked them why they weren't going for Karen Bardsley, who was the England goalkeeper at the time. Matt also represented KB, and he said he'd have a word with Gav. She was about to go to America but she was unbelievable and I probably kind of forced that transfer!

I think I was asking all these questions to try and put off the actual decision. Because it was effectively a start-up and a massive risk. When I moved to Arsenal, nobody was ever going to question my decision because they'd won so much, they'd got all these players, they'd already got the set-up.

Going from a place where they've done it time and time again, a place which was a dream come true for me, to something totally unknown was a massive call.

We started to talk about the contract. It would be for three years, not one, and it would be £24,000 – double what I was on at Arsenal. City would also pay for my accommodation. I could actually start paying into a private pension and I could start to save properly for a deposit because I would not be paying rent for an apartment or a house.

The housing allowance was unbelievable, and it just changed everything. I could concentrate on being a footballer and not have to worry about money.

I obviously spoke to my mam and dad about it. Dad told me that it was absolutely my decision, but I do think he was excited by the fact it was Man City. He thought that this was an opportunity that wasn't going to come around again. That was the thing for me: if I didn't move now, they're just going to get someone else.

How City made me feel was also a big deal. Arsenal never made me feel like I wasn't important, but to know that you'd be a leader in something and be part of it for a long, long time – deep down, I knew I was going to go.

I just needed to figure it out and give myself time. I called Matt at 9 p.m. one night and told him to tell Gav: 'I'm coming.'

It was a really hard decision, because I was happy where I was, but for me as a person as well as a player it was the right move to make.

That's not to say I didn't have any sleepless nights about it, because I did. I felt guilty. I'm a loyal person, so when I'm committed to something I'm committed – whether that's friends, family, whatever. I want to give absolutely everything, and those conversations made me feel a bit uneasy. I remember Shelley once asking where I'd been the day before and I told her I'd been to Manchester but said that I had gone to meet some of my family. I really didn't want to lie, I'd rather just be honest with people. I think she knew. She made a crack about it being a long way to go on a day off. It wasn't a nice part of it at all.

Once I knew Toni, Jill, Izzy and KB were going to City, I knew that we would have a great spine and that we would all be committed for a long time. If we could add a few more people through the next year we wouldn't be far off where we needed to be.

Arsenal got wind and increased their offer, and nearly matched City's, with Matt doing the negotiations. But he had made them aware that I was speaking to other clubs, and a lot of people from that Arsenal team were speaking to other clubs, as people weren't 100 per cent happy.

That maybe swayed my decision as well. I wasn't definite about who was going to be staying next year. There were a lot of big players talking about leaving, so that was another thing to think about. If I stayed at Arsenal it wouldn't necessarily be the same team.

Matt asked me if I had phoned Shelley yet and I told him I hadn't. He told me that I needed to, but I couldn't bring myself to do it. Two hours later I went to the supermarket to distract myself and he messaged me again, saying I needed to phone her. I remember sitting in the car, and I must have been there for half an hour, forty-five minutes, just thinking, You need to do this.

So I called Shelley, from the Colney Sainsbury's car park. I think she could tell I was nervous, and I was just like, 'Look, Shelley, you know that I really appreciate everything you've done.' I was nearly crying but I tried to do it as well as I possibly could. I told her that Arsenal were amazing, a great club and they'd been brilliant for me but I needed to make a change and try something different. I don't think I mentioned that I was going to City, but she knew. She asked if there was anything they could do to change my mind. I told her it was nothing to do with the club, it was nothing to do with her, it was about me. I rehearsed that phone call so many times. It was like ending a relationship.

Because Shelley trusted me and wanted to improve me, she had taken time and effort to make me a better player, which made it really hard. She'd seen things in me that other people might not have done in terms of leadership. She gave me that opportunity and I will always be grateful for that. But football was just changing so quickly, and I didn't want to miss out.

I think Vic had an idea, to be honest, because I hadn't signed the contract for next season. Matt kept going backwards and forwards, saying we just need a bit more time.

I phoned Vic, then met him the next day. I felt as though I needed to go face to face with him.

I just wanted to get it all out there. And I did feel a lot lighter after the phone calls. When there's something like that weighing on your mind, you need to just get it out there, and to have it all done in one night was quite good, but at the same time, you still can't help but feel guilty.

Vic wasn't best pleased. His life is Arsenal, and I don't think he could understand wanting to go somewhere else. He knew potentially there were going to be a few people leaving and obviously he was the guy that signed players and brought people to the club, and he had done so much for the club. It was his baby, really. And I did feel as though I was letting him down but that's the way the game was going. It wasn't just about playing for the best team and playing the best football; there was a lot more to it than just that side. It wasn't just a sport that people played for the enjoyment of it any more, like when I started playing for Sunderland and we were paying to play.

There was a lot more in terms of how you live and what you were worth and whether you were going to be able to earn proper money. All these things had to be taken into consideration given the age I was, whereas when you're young, you just want to play for the best team.

I signed the contract in December, and on 1 January 2014 I became a Manchester City player.

CITY LIGHTS

It wasn't crazy money but I remember getting my first pay packet from City, going to the cash machine and thinking, What the fuck?

My dad was already all over me! Making sure I stayed level-headed. He told me I could have a new car, but that was it. Arsenal had given us a Vauxhall Corsa, which I returned when I left. I'd always liked BMW 1 Series, but I never thought I would have one. It was my one luxury purchase – £200 a month!

I also took my mam, dad and brother out for a meal, which was a first! It was nothing major – we went to Martinos, which is an Italian restaurant near home and it wasn't expensive – but just to be able to say 'I'll get it' was really nice. They didn't know I was going to pay for it. I'd just told them I'd booked a table, and I asked Mam and Dad to try and be amicable because things still weren't great between them. Stuart was amazing because he could break the ice a little bit. My dad had a few pints, and my mam had a bit of wine. I think the whole thing cost about £80 or £90, and while it was only a little thing it was nice to give them something back after all they had done for me.

Other than that, I knew I needed to be sensible. Dad and Matt were really good, helping me plan so I could put money away for a mortgage and pay into a pension. I look at some of the young girls now, who just go and spend everything they earn on clothes and whatever, which is fine, but I was like, no, I need to save.

Soon after I joined, we went to La Manga for a training camp and, to be honest, it was a bit of a shambles. How we ever came out of that to where the club is now is unbelievable. At the time there was five or six of us training full time, and when we got back from Spain we would go to Platt Lane, which was the training ground for the youth teams before the academy opened.

The way that City played at the time, the men's team, was so technical. It was lots of different patterns, so to be able to learn that was unbelievable, but it was very difficult. The City way is that they want all teams playing the same way, from academy to women to men. The idea was that we would train as a five or a six at Platt Lane by ourselves or with the manager on a Monday because we had no games at the weekend, because we were still preseason, and we would go and train with the Under 18 boys.

It was tough. We had been promised this professional

set-up but because a lot of our players were part time we were having to wait till 7 p.m. to train because that was when they finished work, university or college. Nick was a great coach, but the standard just wasn't where it needed to be. It wasn't at the level of Jill, Izzy, KB, Toni and me.

I could totally understand what they were trying to do. They wanted to be loyal to the girls who had played for City for a while. They wanted to give them an opportunity because they did have some good young players. But those first sessions were tough.

The full-timers would train in the morning and then the same evening on the nights that the part-timers were in. So you'd come in for training and then either go back to the apartment in the city centre, which was half an hour away, or to the Starbucks around the corner. We ended up spending half our lives in that Starbucks! Nick, and the sports scientist and our physio, would even come with us.

There were, however, lots of positives in those early days. We had our breakfast at the training ground, which was a big step up from Arsenal. And even walking into the training venue, you could see that the standards were high. There were lots of rules. We were told how to behave as Manchester City players. You had to have your socks pulled up, your shirt tucked in. Every time you went into the canteen or the office and you saw someone, you had to high-five them, give them a fist bump or say good morning.

We even had a meeting where they outlined what was expected of us. I thought that was brilliant. We couldn't really go in and make up our own rules. This was their building, and they were one of the top academies in the country. We learned from them, we abided by their rules and that did us no harm. In fact, there are things that I won't forget, should I ever go into management. Like your water bottle at the side of the pitch – it had to be standing up and in place. If you had to take your jumper off, it had to be folded on the side so everything was tidy. It was smart. We were ready to train. Obviously, there were other rules, such as being on time and respecting your coaches. When you were in the gym you had to make sure you put everything away. Don't leave any bars out, don't leave any dumbbells out. You leave it as you find it, that kind of thing.

Once you're in an environment where you've got a lot of young players coming in on a lot of money, I think it's important you have these rules and it was good for us to fit in.

They had us training with the Under 18s on Mondays, which was an eye-opener. Jason Wilcox, who is now at Manchester United, was the manager and he gave us some really hard sessions. It made no difference that we were women, there was a real respect there.

Some of the talent they had in that building was incredible. There was a kid in there, I think he was fourteen or fifteen, called Phil Foden. Even then he would run rings around me. All the lads were amazing. They were respectful, I think because of what we'd achieved with England. That's what I loved about City: you weren't looked down upon because you were female. It was just people viewing you in terms of what you'd achieved and the person that you were. Jason was very good with the boys, that they would always be humble. They would always come and say hello. But when it got to training, there were no prisoners. It was full contact and it was competitive, and that made me improve so much.

For the women, technically we were probably on the same level as them, but they were a lot faster. So that meant that we had to move the ball quicker. We had to learn to get into position earlier. And it gave us a bit of a challenge to be able to keep up with them. Phil – I mean, you could tell he was going to be a superstar, just by the way he moved, really. He glided across the pitch and his touch – everyone says that about him now, his touch – but his dribbling, his turning, his technique. He was also the first one on the pitch practising, playing keepy-ups, playing it off the wall, playing with whoever was there, and you'd have to fight to get him off the pitch. When he was in possession – and bear in mind, you've got people like Tosin Adarabioyo, who is six foot and Phil is shorter than me – he would give as good as he got. With Phil, you could tell he just loved the game and had really good coaches around him to be able to help him on his way. For us to be a part of that was pretty special.

The good thing about City was that no matter who you got coached by, the principles were still the same, just possibly said in a different way.

Those principles were clear. You need to be technically really good. You need to take pride in your passing. Your touch needed to be spot on. You needed to understand the patterns of play and have respect for everybody else's positions. But, most importantly, you needed to control everything. Whether that's when we have the ball or when we don't have the ball, we need to make sure we are in control. And you have to play good, attractive football.

I feel as though that was my first time I got properly coached in the sense of tactics and patterns. What was expected of my position. Fine details, like giving a little bit of depth to players that you're passing to, to make it harder for the opposition. Honestly, the amount we learned in that first year was absolutely crazy.

We played the Under 18s every Monday until we started to play friendlies. We also did a few sessions with the Under 14s and there was a kid called Cole Palmer who stood out. He and Foden were the ones the coaches always spoke about.

Both of them played in exactly the same positions then as they do now. They were both absolutely ridiculous. And don't get me wrong, it was so competitive. The team that got beaten had to go out and run, so you didn't want that to be you. They were mixed teams, which was good: I think we would have done OK against the lads, but it was good for us to play with different players and have a bit of competitiveness. It set you up for a great week of training. You were so tired after it.

Before the season started, I was feeling pretty confident. We had Toni, who was a striker and who could play anywhere across the front three. She was from Everton, and a massive name at the time. So for her to be the first ever signing for City was a big coup: when you get players of her stature to move, it was like, they mean business. Toni was starting to come into the England set-up as well. We knew that she had unbelievable quality and we needed goals.

Jill was next. I know I'm biased because I've known her all my life, but you want someone like Jill in your team. Her personality, her experience, her ability. We needed someone like that in midfield. Someone in the middle of the pitch that wasn't afraid to get stuck in and could run all day. We also had Izzy Christiansen, who was more technical than Jill. You could see that she had potential to get into the England side, and then there was KB, who was the one for me. I was like, if we are going to have any success, we need the best keeper in the country.

The training stepped up the closer we got to the season starting. You think you know football, and then you come to Man City. I didn't know football. It changed my mindset. Previously, when I was playing a pass, I just played the pass to the person that was free. City got me to understand why we play certain passes and what we're trying to do to opponents.

We even worked on positioning in the box for defending a cross. It was all about the positioning of everyone and how you organise. The reasons why we do certain stuff. It's basic detail that probably everybody sees every single week watching football, but to learn and to practise it was huge. It blew my mind. Football is simple, at the end of the day, if you get those little things right. The level of detail was like nothing I had ever been coached before.

Our first game was Reading in the FA Cup. We won 2–1. Toni scored twice but we didn't play very well. Then we went to Liverpool and we were live on television. Liverpool were the champions and we only lost 1–0. I actually thought we played all right, but you never want to lose your first league game. Then we lost the next game at home to Bristol and we played Doncaster away in the cup. I remember thinking that we'd taken their place in the league and we just couldn't lose against them. We knew that they would be gunning for us. We played so, so bad. They beat us 2–1. It was embarrassing.

The next day we'd planned a brunch at Moose Coffee in town. That was our go-to brunch place. There was me, Jill, Izzy, KB, our physio, our sports scientist and the manager, Nick. And I can just remember us all going, 'What the fuck is going on?' Like what can we do? How can we get better?

We can't afford to lose another game. I actually rang Matt and asked him if there was a release clause in my contract if we got relegated. It was that bad. I thought I'd slipped up here. That I'd made a massive mistake by leaving Arsenal to come to this place. I didn't know where a win was going to come from. It just wouldn't click.

I was also worried about my place in the England squad. I'd been having conversations about becoming England captain and I was thinking that relegation would kill it. I knew I couldn't be playing for a team that was losing every single week. Mark Sampson had replaced Hope and I thought he wasn't going to look at me and think I'm the one to lead an England team to a World Cup or whatever it might be if my team is losing all the time. You have all these thoughts going through your head.

Something had to change. The academy director was a man called Mark Allen and he started to really invest in the women's side. He stripped it back and he knew that if we were going to be successful, we would need the whole team to be full time. I'll never forget this – he agreed to fund it from the academy budget. He took a risk on us and it paid dividends.

Fortunately, we won the next game, at the Etihad against Everton. We scraped a 1–0 win and started to pick up confidence. Sometimes it just takes a little bit of luck to turn things around.

Having said that, the City chairman, Khaldoon Al

Mubarak, came to watch our first home game v Arsenal and we got absolutely battered, 4–0. I remember thinking, He's here, having spent all this money on this women's team, and they're useless. We got our revenge in the August, beating them 1–0 on my first trip back to Borehamwood, when we were growing more as a team.

Before our stadium was ready, we played at the regional athletics place next to the Etihad, which was fine, but having a running track around the pitch wasn't great for atmosphere.

But we got used to it and results started to improve. We finished fifth in the league, and we managed to get to the Continental Cup Final (the League Cup had been renamed after its sponsor, Continental Tyres) to play against Arsenal. I'd got a lot of stick that year for moving, and the noise got louder in the first half of the season because of our results. But we picked up in the second half, signed some good young players including Keira Walsh, and once we had been working together with the manager for four or five months, we came on a lot. In that final we had a few injuries and suspensions, and a really, really young team. I was just thinking in terms of trying to keep the score down. Defend well and hope KB has an absolute blinder of a game.

I got some grief from the Arsenal fans – the game was at Wycombe, so it was a lot closer to them – and there was a bit of hype around the fact I was playing against my old club.

We got absolutely battered in the first half but KB kept us in it, and we grew in confidence. I hit the bar before Izzy nodded one in right from a training-ground move. We ended up winning 1–0 and, as captain, I went up to lift the trophy.

I can't remember too much about the celebrations because I got absolutely smashed. I'm not a massive drinker but it felt right that we enjoyed it. We were on the bus on the way home and Mark Allen, who had invested so much, said that somebody needed to go to the shop and get some drink in. All of a sudden there's wine, beer, everything. I'm useless at an after party and I was drunk after a couple. There's bottles all over the floor and I end up with glass in my foot. We're all at the back, drunk, and we're trying to get this glass out. I was telling them it didn't matter because I'd no games for a few months. I think we ended up out until 4 a.m. and the club arranged taxis to get us all home. That's when I knew that City knew how to party.

They then organised a celebration meal in town. I ended up getting put in a taxi at the end of that too.

I was happy. It felt like vindication that, while it hadn't been the best opening season, I'd made the right decision. We were moving in the right direction. To have the first trophy in the cabinet was massive.

SKIPPER

The 2013 Euros were a disaster. I got injured just before the tournament. Arsenal were playing Chelsea, I was in midfield and Eni Aluko just caught me and I rolled my ankle. I went to St George's Park, where England are based, to do three or four weeks of intensive rehab, and I managed to just about make it, but I knew I wasn't right. When it kicked off, I hadn't played for eight weeks and hadn't really trained with the girls. I needed more game time but there was just no way of getting it. I was grateful to Hope Powell for sticking by me, but with hindsight I think I came back too soon.

Even so, we'd had an amazing Olympics and were all pretty confident when we set off for Sweden. But from the start it was a bit off. It felt flat and it's difficult to explain why. It just felt like we were trapped. We were in the same hotel for four or five weeks, I was rooming with Ellen, which was great, but it felt like you couldn't really

129

escape. Whereas normally, during a tournament, you move between hotels, cities, towns, for this one we were literally stuck and there wasn't much to keep us occupied. Every day felt the same. The place was remote. We were beside a river, so in terms of scenery it was pretty. But there's only so long you can look out of the window.

I think pressure played a part too. It was the first tournament where as a team we felt that we were expected to go and do something, because we'd climbed the rankings and done well at London 2012.

There was criticism of our playing style, but the fact was that we just didn't play well. I mean, we only managed one point and finished bottom of our group, so clearly something went wrong.

We never really got hold of a game. The sport was getting very tactical and I'm not sure we were ready for that.

But it's hard to blame anyone except for ourselves. As players we had to take responsibility because we weren't good enough, both individually and collectively. We had so much experience and so much potential, but the other teams had probably worked us out. Physically, they were also able to match up, which took away one of our strengths.

None of us had any idea that it would be the end for Hope. England without her just seemed weird but the FA decided to make a change. I can't speak highly enough of Hope. Not just for me, but what she's done for the game – she's been absolutely unreal. She has been a pioneer. On a personal level, I couldn't have asked for any more of her, not only as a manager but also as a person. She always came back to me after my injuries, kept her word and showed unbelievable faith in me. She recognised my potential and she allowed me to grow. She persisted with me, which I'll be forever grateful for.

She was also honest. We used to have training camps in La Manga, which were brutal. At the end of them she would cut the squad down. She once told me straight at the end of the week that I hadn't made the cut, and I'd be flying home. I asked her what I needed to do to improve. She told me she needed me back at the level I was at previously. 'Just do what you need to do,' she said. I actually appreciated it. Sometimes I feel as if managers don't have that honesty. She was right: I was coming back from an injury and didn't have the rhythm. I wasn't where I should have been.

I also loved her as a coach. You knew exactly what she wanted from you. She was straight to the point, no matter who you were, and she did not suffer fools. I liked that, because there were some superstars in that team. She kept you on your toes and you knew when she wasn't happy, but you would always be desperate to impress her.

Looking back, maybe she'd taken us as far as she possibly could. She had been in charge for fifteen years, and after the way that we went out and performed in Sweden, she probably thought it was time for somebody else to come in.

I was disappointed, but I got it. I couldn't have asked for a better manager when I was younger, or for someone that was able to guide me in the right direction. Trust in football is massive and I feel as though she did really trust me. And I like to think that I give her that back in my performances and my training and my attitude. Hope had an aura about her, and I'll never forget that she gave me my debut when there were so many other players she could have chosen.

Even these last couple of years, when it's been really tough from an international point of view, she was one of the first people to reach out and tell me that she was there if I needed her. She knew I'd be feeling alone. I still talk to her now and take advice about my future. When you're fortunate enough to know people like that it's important that you listen to them.

When I was considering retirement, I asked her a lot about what the next steps are, because it is quite scary when you're coming to the end of your career. Hope knows me, and she told me to just be true to myself. She's always offered me the opportunity to coach if that's what I want to do.

The FA went for Mark Sampson to replace Hope, and I was happy with that because I'd always been impressed by his Bristol sides, who were well organised and hard to beat. I'd had some big battles with them over the years.

But I was still shitting myself for his first squad

announcement. After the Euros I lost my place at left-back under the caretaker manager Brent Hills, who had told me I needed to play centre-half. I wasn't able to do that until my first year at City, so I was nervous about making it, but the squad was announced for the January training camp in La Manga and I was in it.

Mark had arranged one-on-one meetings with everyone in the group – which must have been about thirty of us – and I asked my dad for advice. He told me to just answer what I was asked, and to be honest. Explain why I moved to City, what the thinking was and make it clear how important it is for me to keep my England place.

I kind of knew Mark liked me from his Bristol days, because every time I played against him he was like, 'Fuck's sake, not you again!' which I guess was affectionate. He was always really complimentary after games when I played for Arsenal, and I thought he was a great appointment because I knew he was good at getting the best out of his players.

In our meeting, he got straight to the point and asked me to explain why I'd gone to City. He also asked me what I thought my best position was. I told him about the project at City and how I was sure that we'd be a success, and I said that I honestly didn't know what my best position was because I'd played all over the place. I also said I preferred centre-half because I thought that gave me the best chance of making the squad.

He agreed, and then said he wanted to talk to me about

leadership. I had no idea where he was going with it. I think I even asked him what he meant! He asked me what I was like as a leader, what I brought to the team. I told him that I lead by example in terms of how I train, how I am around gym sessions and in and around the building. I felt it was a little bit weird that he was asking that, because I was twenty-five, quite a new captain of Man City and I'd only captained Arsenal for maybe half a season.

He told me that we had two games coming up and he wanted me to be captain for one of them. What the fuck? I've gone from being grateful to be picked to thinking I might be captain. I never, ever imagined in a million years that I would be anywhere near a leadership position because of the experience that we had in the squad. I asked, 'Really?' and Mark told me he wanted to see how I went, and to relax and enjoy it. We played against Norway in my game, and as captain I presented the pendant to the Norway captain before the match. To see the pendant hanging on my peg in the dressing room kind of brought it home to me.

I took a picture and sent it to my brother, who put it on Facebook. I was buzzing, but probably more because I knew that the new manager rated me rather than thinking I was going to replace Casey Stoney.

I led the team out and we had a huddle. We would do a lot of huddles, and the captain would always speak first, just out of respect. Mark wanted things done a certain way to bring togetherness, to bring that team ethos, which was a new way of us all working together. That was also the first time I'd played properly for England in centre-back for a long time. So to be given that armband and that new position was unbelievable.

We went to the Cyprus Cup in March, and I did two games as captain and Fara Williams did two. We won the tournament and had another camp at St George's Park in April. None of us were any the wiser about what the captaincy decision would be. We had a meeting before tea one night and Mark said he would let us know in the next few days.

I was rooming with Ellen, as always, and I got a message from Mark asking me to come down to reception. I've just had a shower, I'm in my pyjamas and I'm about to get in bed because we were going to watch an episode of *Breaking Bad*. But I go down and Mark's just sitting there on a couch in the hotel foyer. I looked like a tramp with my wet hair.

Anyway, he asked me how I thought I'd done, asked me if I was enjoying life at City, and then asked me what I'd bring if I was England captain.

I told him I'd try to lead by example in everything that I did. I'd put the girls first as much as I possibly could and I'd wear my heart on my sleeve because that's what I do every single day. And then he asked me if I wanted to be England captain.

I had to ask him to repeat himself, and when he did, I

asked him if he was joking. I think he might have laughed but he told me he thought I was the right age, in the right position and was going to be the spine of the team for the next however many years.

I couldn't even tell you what happened in the rest of the conversation. He told me he was going to announce it to the girls tomorrow in a meeting, and not to tell anyone.

I was like, 'Can I tell my mam and dad?' He laughed again and said I could, but they couldn't tell anyone, and then said 'Night, skip.' That was the first time anyone had ever called me skip.

As I walked back to my room I was buzzing but I was also wondering what everyone else would think.

At the back of my mind I was thinking, This is not going to go down too well. But at the same time, I couldn't stop smiling. I told Ellen I'd just been to see the doc and then I found somewhere quiet, called my dad and told him. 'Fuck off!' he said. I told him I wasn't joking. He was delighted, said that was amazing and that he was so proud of me. I rang Mam, who didn't really know what it meant, but she started crying down the phone. And my brother was like my dad, telling me he was proud of me.

Mark announced it the next day in a team meeting. I got a round of applause and then he asked me if I wanted to say anything. He put me on the spot because I'm not a massive public speaker and my mind went blank. I just said it was a massive honour to lead the group and to follow in the footsteps of some amazing people. I said I wanted to make everyone proud and that I was there for them, and that was kind of it.

Mark pushed me out of my comfort zone straight away, which he did quite a lot. He kept pushing and challenging.

My first game as captain was against Montenegro at Brighton and all the family came down. No disrespect to Montenegro, but it was a good opponent to ease myself into the role and we won 9–0.

The only downside had been the night before the game, when my phone started ringing at 1 a.m. It was the physio at City. By then I'd left the apartment in the city centre and me and KB had moved into a house the club had found for us in Withington. I went out into the corridor because I didn't want to wake Ellen and called the physio back.

She told me that we'd been burgled. KB was injured and so she wasn't in the squad, but fortunately she'd been out. They ransacked the place, took a Gucci watch that I got as a present, my speakers, headphones and KB's laptop, but they'd not found the keys to my new car, which was outside on the street. After being told I was captain and then getting that call I was an emotional wreck. It's a day I won't forget in a hurry.

Stephanie Jayne Houghton.
Born on 23 April 1988

With my brother Stuart, wearing our South
Hetton Primary School uniforms, keeping up
a birthday tradition with a Sunderland cake

Me, my dad Len, my mam
Amanda and Stu on holiday.
No matter what, family
always comes first

A dream come true:
Sunderland Easter football
ap, wearing my England 96
kit, getting scouted for my
team, Sunderland

All I ever wanted to do was
wear the red and white strip

England World Cup debut v France
in the quarter-final

This time was a definite YES to signing for the Arse
My first FA Cup trophy with the Gooners

It's been some journey with
Jill Scott, from Sunderland
Centre of Excellence to scoring
and playing for England. I would
have her in my team every time

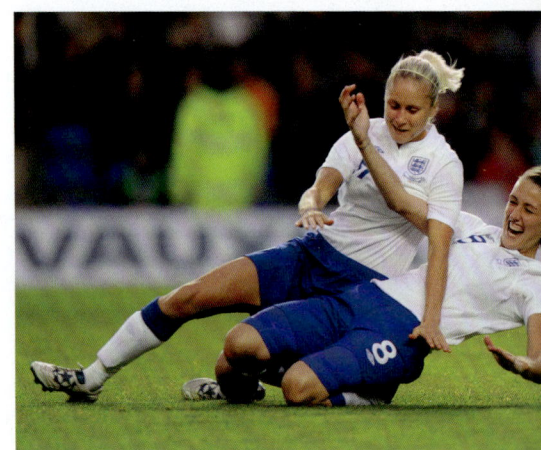

that Brazil goal. Still to this day I don't know why I was in the box or how it went in

I'm under there somewhere. The sound of that packed-out Wembley crowd supporting Team GB and this amazing team is still unforgettable. Life changing

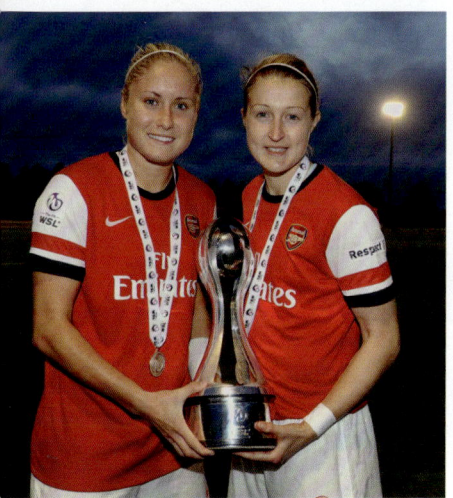

Ellen White, my roommate and one of my best mates, lifting the WSL title together. That's why we moved to Arsenal

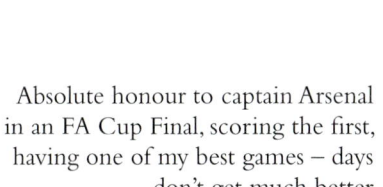

Absolute honour to captain Arsenal in an FA Cup Final, scoring the first, having one of my best games – days don't get much better

History makers: World Cup 2015. We wanted to inspire a nation, and we certainly did.
Winning bronze against the odds, a team that was together no matter what

WSL league champions. Three years
of work in a project we all believed in
finally came together in 2016

Steph Houghton, MBE, for services to football.
Never in a million years would I have thought
of receiving such honour. The most special day
with my family at Buckingham Palace

Playing in the Champions League
semi-final for City against Lyon, one of
the most dominant teams. We were so
close but yet so far

One of the biggest FA Cup upsets in history. Skipper Darby leading Bradford to a 4–2 victory against Didier Drogba's Chelsea at Stamford Bridge. So proud

Sharon Latham

Mr and Mrs Darby,
21-06-2018

BEST day of my life:
rying my soulmate

John Dewhirst

At the first official Darby Rimmer MND Foundation fundraiser, a match between two of Stephen's old clubs, Bradford v Liverpool at Valley Parade. ootball came together to show Stephen he will never walk alone

2019 Continental Cup winners.
A trophy I loved lifting

Climbing the steps of Wembley
do what so many previous capta
have done before in the FA C

Captaining England: eight
years of pure pride. The great
honour and privilege

That penalty miss, and
semi-final heartbreak again.
Devastated. Me and the boss,
Phil Neville. I owe a lot to him,
he really understood how to
treat me as a player and a person
to get the best out of me

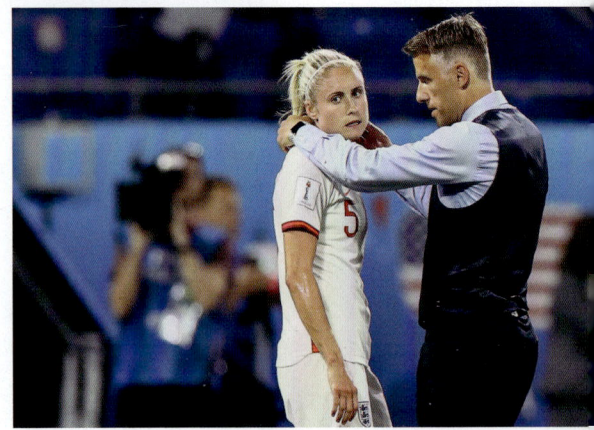

Signing another contract extension with my team, Manchester City, with the help of Matthew Buck. My agent but now one of mine and Stephen's closest friends. Thank you for everything you have done in changing women's football, but also for me – wouldn't have done it without you

With Nick Cushing, celebrating a derby day win v United. Nick, as a coach you changed me as a player and a leader

Lynne Cameron

My Achilles hell. Doing everything I can to get fit and ready for Euro 2020, but sacrificing everything ended in heartache

Back to my best form, beating Arsenal at home. I missed this feeling

My final ever game, v Aston Villa away. Overcome by emotion from both sets of fans. This game has given me so much throughout my career. I will always be eternally grateful for the career I have had

The most amaz
send-off from my C
family at my final ho
game, after announc
my retirement. I l
this c

My family. Through the ups and downs they have always been there to share the journey with me. I love you all

JET-LAGGED AND BROKEN

We had really high hopes going into the 2015 World Cup. We'd qualified well, and the FA paid for us all to go out to Canada business class, which was another example that times were changing.

We didn't get off to a great start, with the old enemy France beating us 1–0 in the first group game, but I thought that there were lots of positives to take from it.

We won our next three games – I scored in the last one against Norway – to put us into the quarter-final against the hosts.

I can honestly say I have never played in an atmosphere as hostile as what faced us in Vancouver. There were fifty-five thousand people there and it sounded like every single one of them wanted us to lose. It was crazy but I absolutely loved it. There isn't anything like going into that kind of environment and silencing it. That lack of noise when we knocked Canada out 2–1 was perfect.

Japan were next, in the semi-final, and we thought we had a great chance. We kind of cancelled each other out. They had a lot of the ball, but we were never in any danger. But after about half an hour they got a ludicrous penalty when Claire Rafferty shoved Saori Ariyoshi. It was a foul – but it was at least a yard outside the area. Ridiculous.

About five minutes later we were attacking, and I felt contact from behind me. I got a bit of grief on social media afterwards for the way I went down but she took my boot clean off my foot. It was a foul, we got the penalty, Fara scored it and we were level before half-time.

In the second half we had the upper hand and Toni Duggan smashed a volley against the bar. It was the best we'd played in the tournament. We were getting better every game, and we felt like we were in the ascendant, but we couldn't find the goal. I was getting ready for extra time when they attacked down the right.

I can see the ball coming in now, and I went across to deal with it but before I could get there Laura Bassett, who had her back to me, moved in. We'd played alongside each other so often and we knew each other's games. I felt like she was in control.

Honestly, it could have gone anywhere when she stuck her leg out. But it looped over KB, hit the bar and came down over the line. I had a great view of it, and I knew it was in, but I ran over and hooked it clear just in case. The ref gave the goal and I can remember thinking, This just couldn't be worse. We had no time whatsoever to come back.

Bass was distraught, in tears, and I was devastated for her. I'd known her for so long, she was probably my favourite centre-half partner in my whole career. She was great when I was coming through and everyone in the squad looked up to her. When the whistle went, I wasn't even thinking about missing out on the final. I just knew this was my friend, that it would really hurt her and that she would blame herself. She'd had an unbelievable tournament, and we won as a team and we lost as a team.

We would usually have a debrief but Mark told us to forget that. To go away and switch off. Recover, because we had Germany in the bronze match three days later.

At the time we'd been working with a sports psychologist, and he was big on getting me to only focus on the things that I could control.

After I got the captaincy, there were maybe a few questions asked within the group, and also by the public. Maybe she's a little bit too young, hasn't got enough experience, that type of thing. And when you say you don't read all that kind of stuff, well you do. I read it and my family are telling me about it as well. Maybe it's a bad thing, but I think it's better to know than not to know. So I think I tried to be everybody's mate. I tried too hard when I was playing, instead of concentrating on what I was learning at

City and what I was learning at England. The manager and the staff had shown great faith in terms of giving me the opportunity. And I think Mark was really good at sensing things. He knew when I wasn't really being myself. So we brought a psychologist in, who massively influenced my career and the way that I am as a person, and brought back things that I didn't really think about myself. I remember him sitting down with me and asking what I wanted to be as a captain. Obviously, I wanted to lead by example. I wanted to show that I cared for people. This was at St George's. But he would always have to pull me in for a chat. I would never go to him, and I think that was his biggest bugbear – I should have really approached him.

At first, I wouldn't really talk. He asked me to strip down what I wanted to be as a captain, but also what I wanted to be as a player. Having those conversations, those hard conversations, was exactly what I needed at the time.

I wasn't really open, but he had such a special way of letting me explain how I felt. And obviously, the player that I am, I always pressure myself to be the best, and I wanted to be the best straight away, whereas I need to realise it was going to be a bit of a journey, I was going to make mistakes along the way, and it was going to be uncomfortable at times. But the only person I needed to prove myself to was me. I didn't need to prove myself to anybody else.

The way it worked in camp, we would train, we would have meetings, I would be called in for leadership meetings,

I would never really have time for myself. I was here, there and everywhere, so the psychologist got me to write down what I could control. We called it the bubble.

Before the third-place game against Germany I wrote down what my jobs were attacking, what my jobs were defensively, and what my leadership duties were. And I put them in a bubble of, like, OK, this is what I can control. To see it on a piece of paper really helped me focus on stuff. But also, on the outside of the bubble, I had the media, fans, family, my teammates, the manager. They were things I really couldn't control. I had a little book, and every time I went into a meeting, I'd write all these notes down. Tactics, this was my way of preparing, knowing I had all this information. So, before I put my tracksuit on, I'd sit down on my bed and I put my bubble in this book. I'd rip the page out, go and get a shower, go to the game, and I'd always have the piece of paper in my bag. On the way to the stadium, I'd read the piece of paper, and that was my way of being able to develop but also concentrate on myself instead of thinking about what everybody else thought of me.

That really had a massive influence on how I developed as a leader, my communication style, and how I could be with people. And also the psychologist was really positive, which helped me. I really got more confident with the positivity and the feedback that I had, because sometimes in these environments, you don't really get as much feedback as you probably should. And, being captain, you don't get it from the girls. I needed to lean on the staff a little bit more, to have them say that I'd done a good job here, or maybe I could do that a little bit there. So in terms of that journey, that was probably the biggest influence in terms of leadership that I had.

The bronze match was tough, which it was always going to be against Germany. We'd not beaten them for thirty-one years and they'd battered us at Wembley the last time we'd played them, so we weren't exactly confident.

That whole tournament was mad in that we changed formation every single game. Every formation for every team was different. I don't think we had the same starting eleven, either. And then to go up against Germany and play a 5–4–1 that we'd never, ever played before in the biggest game of the tournament felt absolutely insane. For the first five or ten minutes, we got peppered, and it was a scorching day.

But there was a mentality about us. We were desperate to get a win, and I think what had happened against Japan, and with Laura, was behind that. We should never, ever have lost to Japan and that seriously stung us. They should never have had a penalty, and there was that freak own goal. After that game, everybody was absolutely heartbroken, but also angry, so emotional. I was like, We're going to win this next one. No matter what, we will find a way to win. We couldn't change what had happened, but we could change what is in front of us. We could see how gutted Bass was and the effect it had on her. She's one of my oldest friends and we had been through so much together. We wanted to do whatever we could to give her a lift and get her out of that place she was in. I actually think that, as a team, it brought us together. We became even more motivated to go and beat Germany. We were desperate for it.

I think they kind of expected to beat us off the back of that Japan game, that we would still be feeling the aftereffects and just wanted to get ourselves home. So for all that the change of formation was hard for us as players, we adapted really well. I cleared one off the line in the first ten minutes and thought, We can't keep doing this. But we somehow managed to get it to extra time, and then you're wondering how on earth we're going to get through another thirty minutes. Can we even last?

Then Lianne Sanderson comes on and wins us the penalty, and Fara Williams steps up and scores it. And then, well, unbelievable scenes, to be honest. It meant so much. We were elated not just for ourselves but for Laura too. It was a weird mix of elation and relief. They had done us 3–0 at Wembley and nobody expected us to win after what had happened against Japan. We might not have won the tournament, but we ended up the highest-placed team from Europe and to finally beat the Germans after thirty-one years felt like a huge step forward.

We were absolutely knackered and had left everything

out there. I honestly don't think the FA expected us to get as far as we did, so plans to bring us back in business class were never in place. For me, the justification for the expense was there. We'd got past the group stage and we ended up winning the bronze medal. But then we're told we're coming back economy – and don't forget that we're in the middle of the season, so we were going straight back to play for our clubs. It wasn't a bit shit, it was a lot shit. You really don't want to keep comparing yourselves to the men, but you do think they would have probably had a private jet, coming back from winning a bronze medal. But even just to get bonus money for that World Cup was ridiculous. We wanted everyone to be paid, no matter how much they had played, and it was such a struggle. Everyone deserved to be treated the same, but we met some resistance from the FA, which really annoyed me. We were all meant to be in this together.

The leadership group put it to the players that we thought we should all get the same bonus, regardless of how many minutes we had played. We were all members of the England squad and would be ready to perform if called upon.

The girls gave us their backing and told us to just do what we needed to do. It was important that we were unified, we were together, that we were aligned. We told them that we might have to say no to whatever was offered and try and push for more. I would speak to Matt and Marie and Gordon Taylor at the PFA. They were absolutely brilliant in terms of having conversations with higher-ups at the FA. They would talk to them on our behalf, tell them that this is what the players want and this is what's going to happen. In terms of the central contracts, the bonuses, the commercial things that we've got in place now – without the backing of the PFA and people that were experienced enough to do that, I don't think we would have been as far on as we are now.

But we didn't manage to get business class flights home, which was a bit of a killer.

It had been such a long tournament and there was no expectation outside our dressing room. I think that was the thing. The saddest thing about it was that we never ever thought we would get that far. I'm presuming England now fly on a private plane everywhere they go, which is amazing, and rightly so – you're representing the country and people come to watch you play. You sell out Wembley. Why wouldn't you do that? So much was asked of us as players, to be professional and sacrifice all these things, but we weren't really being helped in return. I think that didn't just piss us off in 2015, it pissed the clubs off as well. We went out and worked so hard for seven weeks in Canada and then we had to come back and play about four days later, but they couldn't provide something like a comfortable flight to get us back in some kind of decent shape.

To make it worse, it wasn't even a direct flight. We

played the bronze medal game in Edmonton, so we went from there to I think either Montreal or Toronto. From there, we flew back to London, but obviously a lot of us were needed in Manchester, so we went from London to Manchester by car after we landed. The whole journey took about sixteen hours overnight, without a wink of sleep. It wasn't ideal.

We played Birmingham and somehow managed to win 1–0. Those of us who had been away were absolutely exhausted. We were jet-lagged and broken. Absolutely shot. We'd played seven games, and the last one went for 120 minutes.

DUTCH DISMAY

We were in good shape for the 2017 Euros and sailed through the group stages, winning all three matches against Scotland, Spain and Portugal. I'd got a yellow against Scotland and so I played against Spain on a knife edge, but I was really pleased with the game. Spain were a typical Spanish team. Kept the ball. They had 82 per cent possession throughout the whole game. We had 18 per cent and won 2–0. It chucked it down, the pitch was a bog and we might as well have been in Manchester, not Holland. It was Millie Bright's first tournament and she played alongside me at centre-half. I liked her from the start. She's a northerner who calls it as she sees it, so we obviously had a lot in common. She doesn't give a shit. She plays how she plays.

Millie had presence and her aerial ability was a strength – it's what makes her who she is. In that Spain game we worked so well together. Anything that was in the box, it was only us that was getting a header on it, we were blocking, we were tracking back, and we were so strong. That was probably one of my favourite games because there's no better feeling when, no matter what they try, they aren't scoring.

We had France in the quarter-final. Our record against them wasn't great so we felt like we had scores to settle. It was a really tight game and Jill picked up a yellow card, which meant she would miss the semi-final. After an hour, Lucy Bronze intercepted a ball and went on one of her long runs. She played in Jodie Taylor, who scored her fifth goal of the tournament. I don't think we'd beaten France for forty-three years. We defended for our lives that night.

We had the Netherlands in the semi-final and, to be honest, we just didn't turn up. It wasn't the atmosphere – we'd faced that against Canada and had no issues – we just didn't play well and it was really frustrating.

I absolutely love it when you know you're playing in their backyard, and you know that they don't want you to win or play well. That's probably when I'm at my best, when people don't really want you to do well and are doubting you as a player. And I feel that's been the story of my career, that people have had those doubts, but I've always fought back. I think back to games like Canada in Edmonton. That was probably my favourite game from a World Cup: the boos when we came out to warm up were unbelievable. You just have a feeling inside you where you're like,

OK, we're going to beat them. There was silence when we scored, but when Canada scored just before half-time the noise was deafening. I think in those moments, this is what you want it to be in these environments, in these atmospheres. So I don't feel as though, personally, I was intimidated by that crowd against the Netherlands.

I honestly thought we had a chance of winning that tournament, and by the end of it you're just thinking, Is it ever going to happen? Against Japan, we did everything we could. But in that Netherlands game, we just didn't show the best version of us and lost 3–0. I don't think I had a bad game personally, but it wasn't one of my best and it needed to be that for everyone. For whatever reason, we just didn't really attack in the way we had previously in that tournament. With the players that we had and the experience we had, I really thought we could go the whole way. Before the game, I was actually really interested to see what we were going to do, if we would change without Jill. We spoke about being adaptable quite a lot in the tournament, but we just went out and did pretty much the same thing. I think back now, and maybe having a change in formation would have helped. But we never really got to grips with how they were playing, and the midfield had a bit too much space. I don't think it was our finest performance and we weren't really able to solve the problems. That was probably the most disappointing thing.

It wasn't to be. Then you start wondering what's going

to happen next, with the team and with the manager. Are the FA going to stick with Mark?

On a personal level, he was unbelievable for me. He taught me so much, and of course there were times when he gave me a bollocking, and that was fair. But for him giving me that opportunity to captain the team, to actually have that faith and trust in me not only as a player, but also as a leader, and to learn the things that I did, I will be forever grateful.

STEPHEN

I first met Stephen in a really romantic setting. It was
the 2014 annual general meeting of the Professional
Footballers' Association at the Midland Hotel in
Manchester. I was City's representative, and he was
Bradford's.

We'd literally just finished the season, so I had no excuse
not to go. I didn't want to because I find the things really
boring. There's only so many speeches you can listen to,
and I just haven't got the mental capacity for it. I was moaning to Matt that I wouldn't know anyone, and that I was
going to be there by myself. He said I'd be all right because
Darbs was going. I didn't even know who Darbs was.

So I get there and I'm really nervous because the number
of boys to girls was ridiculous. I was almost the only girl
in the room, and I hate mingling and making small talk.

I was sitting on a couch with Marie when Darbs walked
over. Marie said, 'Doesn't he smell amazing?' Back then

footballers were all wearing this aftershave, Creed Aventus, and to be fair it *did* smell amazing. We were introduced, but then had to go into the main meeting where Gordon Taylor, who was the boss of the PFA back then, spoke for an hour. Me and Stephen were sitting next to each other. We didn't really say much but, I don't know, sometimes you just have a bit of a feeling. And I did think he was quite good looking. We then had to go around in groups to different stations on things like finance and sports management. We did that together and we were getting on, but at that stage it was more just chat about football. He's a Liverpool fan, and he had a proper Scouse accent.

At the end of the meeting he offered to walk me to my car because he's a gentleman. He said his was in the same car park, so it wasn't out of his way. It was only later I found that he'd actually parked about a mile away.

I went back to mine – I was living with KB at the time. She told me I smelled amazing. Stephen had given me a kiss on the cheek goodbye, and she could smell his aftershave on my jacket. I told KB that he was a lovely lad and that I needed to find out whether he was single.

The next day I was going to Ellen White's wedding. I drove down to London from Manchester, and I rang Matt and I rang Marie, trying to gauge whether Darbs had said anything about me.

Marie said she'd just had him on the phone asking if I was single and if he could have my number. Obviously I said yes, and then waited for him to text me. I was never going to be the one to make the first move – and I need to make that clear!

I was with Claire Rafferty at the wedding – we were both bridesmaids – and all these rugby boys that were Ellen's husband's mates, doing shots, when my phone went off.

It was a text from Darbs, who said he'd got my number off Marie and was it OK if he messaged me?

We spent that whole night texting each other. He was playing an away match for Bradford and was in the team hotel. I wondered if he was just texting because he was by himself and bored.

But I had a feeling, and within the first few hours I knew he had the same morals as me, the same values. We were quite similar as players as well, really hard working and dedicated.

It was all going well until he ghosted me! We were texting backwards and forwards for pretty much the whole week, and we spoke about maybe going on a date but nothing came of it because our schedules were just so different.

The next Saturday he had a game, so I messaged him wishing him luck. He messaged back after it, saying he was going on a night out and asking if I was going to James Milner's charity ball in Manchester, which I was. And then that was it. I went to the Christmas markets on the Sunday and there was still no message.

I thought he'd found someone else. Anyway, he eventually sent me a message and said his phone died and he didn't have a charger. I told him not to give me that nonsense, everyone has an iPhone charger, but he was adamant. He still claims that was the case to this day.

Anyway, we finally went out on our first date, which was at Gaucho, a steak restaurant in Manchester. He said he'd come and pick me up, and I was stressing the whole day what to wear. Mam was at mine, and she was asking me what kind of car he drove. I thought it would be a footballer car – I mean, he was captain of Bradford, who are a decent club – but I didn't know. He called to say he was twenty minutes away, so I asked him what car I needed to look out for. He told me a Volkswagen Passat. A Volkswagen Passat. I soon got to know that that was him. He wasn't materialistic in the slightest. He just wanted to play football, go out with the lads and make sure his family were OK.

So we go to Gaucho and that was that, really. He seemed like a proper grown-up. I'd seen boys before, but I'd never been too bothered: I'd rather concentrate on my football. When I think about it now, I just knew Stephen was the one. I had never had that feeling before in my life. People say when you don't search for it, it just comes to you, and it was like that. I certainly never expected to meet someone at the PFA AGM!

Meeting his parents for the first time was a pretty big deal, and I hate what he did to me!

It was a Sunday, and he had the day off. He had his own house, so I went round and he said he'd cook us dinner and we'd chill and watch *Game of Thrones*. We started watching it and he told me he needed to pop to his mum and dad's to pick something up for dinner.

I went with him, I was just in my jeans and I always remember, I didn't have any socks on. I thought I'd stay in the car while he went in and got whatever he needed to get.

Oh no, I was invited in, with no socks on. I was so nervous, but they were amazing. I could see Stephen is the way that he is because of his mum and dad and how they are. They couldn't have been any more welcoming. His dad loves football as much as mine does, so he was peppering me with questions about football. His dad is an Everton fan – I think all the family are, apart from Stephen. His best mate at school was a Liverpool fan and he wouldn't let Stephen in the house unless he said he was a Liverpool supporter too, so he has been one ever since.

His mum was just lovely – and he's definitely a mummy's boy.

I can remember asking if they liked me. As if to say, did they approve? And he told me they absolutely loved me, which was great.

When he met my parents, it was pretty similar. It was in December, in the off season, and he came up to Durham. We had a lovely walk by the river, something to eat and then we went to the pub. When he gave me a lift home I dragged him into the house. He'd done it to me, hadn't he?

My parents loved him. I think my dad likes him because he's got such a dry sense of humour.

We'd go and watch each other's games and critique performances. He was an amazing player. He'd started at Liverpool and been at Bradford for a long time, and while he wasn't a marauding full-back, nobody could get past him. He was ridiculous. I went to Port Vale to watch him, which was glamorous, but I missed the game when they went to Chelsea in the FA Cup and knocked Chelsea out. He's actually lucky we're still together after that weekend because we went to watch *The Lion King* the next day and he fell asleep in the theatre. He was so hungover, and still stank of booze.

I did have reservations about going out with a footballer, especially that first weekend when he didn't text back. I was like, please don't be one of those typical boys that you hear so many stories about. I think I always knew he wasn't, but you don't properly know that until you really get to know someone and you get to know their mates. I just loved the fact that, like for me, everything was about family. He's also really funny, and just one of the nicest people you'll ever meet.

We'd been together for just over two years when we got engaged. I'd been dropping quite a few hints, to be fair. But the more I asked, the more he refused to do it.

A lot of my mates were starting to get engaged, and a lot of my school friends and the girls that I'd grown up with. We'd been to a few weddings, and we had bought a house together, so we were building for the future. Stephen said he had never thought about having kids until he met me, whereas my mindset was always to have a family and to make sure the kids had a similar upbringing to what we had both had.

We had a few disagreements over when we should get engaged. He wanted it to be on his terms, but I was like, I don't want to be thirty when I'm getting married.

We'd had a game on Wednesday, Doncaster away, and the next day was my day off. On Thursday morning, the girls at City were saying that we were going to go and get our nails done, then we'd go to have brunch and have a chill day. Stephen was off at the time, and I'd have preferred to spend the day with him, but he was adamant that I go out with the girls. While I was out, he kept on messaging me, which really wasn't like him. He kept asking what time I was going to be back. I still didn't twig that anything was going on.

Eventually, I pulled up outside the house and saw the living room blinds were down. I was raging. I thought the neighbours would think we were absolute tramps, with the blinds down at 3 p.m.

I opened the door, ready to shout at him, and there were rose petals leading from the hallway to the living room. I asked him what was going on and he just told me to come in and sit down. I could tell he was welling up a bit. He didn't really say much, he just had this book, an album, which was full of photos from when we first met. And he was trying to speak but he was struggling. It was December and we had the Christmas tree up. We looked through the album and he gave me a cuddle. Then he went to the tree, and I was wondering why. He pulled a box out from the tree, and to this day I couldn't even tell you what he said, I was just crying.

I obviously said yes, and we couldn't wait to ring our families and tell them. My dad already knew, because Stephen had asked him while he was on the way to pick up an Indian takeaway.

Everybody was so happy for us. We couldn't wait to build a future together. I did wonder about the timing, though. It turned out it was Stephen's Christmas do the next day and he was going to Winter Wonderland with the lads. I think he might have timed it to keep me sweet!

We then had to arrange our stag and hen dos, because we were going to get married in June. I went to Edinburgh with a load of friends from Durham, my mam, Stephen's mum and my auntie from Scotland – the one who bought me my England kit.

My cousin Amy was my chief bridesmaid, so she organised the whole thing. Phil Neville had become England manager and I had to miss the FA Awards. He never, ever let me forget it.

We went up to Scotland, and then a few of the football girls came up too, like Jill Scott and Laura Bassett. Ellen White was one of my bridesmaids.

There was a good mixture of football and normal friends. On the Friday, we just went out in Edinburgh during the day, had a meal and went to a club after, which was funny. I didn't know what time we got in. And then on Saturday we went to the races at Musselburgh, which was class.

Stephen, on the other hand, went to Dublin and I didn't speak to him for three days.

We agreed on 21 June for the wedding, so we didn't have much time. We wanted somewhere in the North-East, but given our friends were from all over we needed somewhere with loads of rooms and that place just didn't seem to exist. So we started to look in Manchester, because there were hotels everywhere. We settled on a place in Knutsford, called Colshaw Hall. The first time I saw it, I knew it was the place. I could just picture everyone being there. The bridal party could stay the night before, there was a little chapel for us to get married in and the views were out of this world.

It was midsummer day, the longest day of the year, and the weather couldn't have been any better. You talk about perfect days – honestly, all of my friends still talk about it to this day. It was perfect from start to finish.

We had a roast beef dinner. That was our favourite food. Sticky toffee pudding for dessert. Maybe not the best thing on one of the hottest days of the year, but everybody seemed to enjoy it. I also had to have pick and mix, because I love sweets.

We got a photographer from City to do our photos, Sharon Latham, who's a massive character. She wanted a big group shot and everyone was waiting for me. Sharon shouted out, 'Oi, dickhead, get in this picture!' My grandma was amazed. 'Who is this woman?' she said. Everyone was killing themselves laughing. Everyone remembers the photographer.

We thought about naming the tables after stadiums we'd played in, but decided it was a bit pretentious. In our house, we've made a conscious effort not to have it very football. Some people, you go in and there are shirts on the wall straight away. It was the same for our wedding. We thought, OK, we'd rather it just be Steph and Stephen, rather than football. But of course, my dad's speech was about football, and he absolutely caned some of the girls.

He hammered Laura Bassett for what happened at the World Cup, which was a fine line. And we got some stick for the 2017 Euros. He also slammed Stephen and all his mates. Poor Stephen also got it in the neck from his best man, his brother Kevin. He told a story about his mum telling him to be quiet because Stephen had done a double

day – training in the morning and then gym in the afternoon – and was having a lie down.

'I've worked from eight until five,' Kevin said, 'and I've
got to be quiet for Ste, who's "worked" from ten until two.
Unbelievable.'

The speeches were class. I think Stephen cried the whole
way through his. He also cried as soon as I walked down
the aisle.

I wore a white dress: Stephen's Catholic and we wanted
to keep it very traditional.

It was a big day for me, something I'd thought about a
lot. Even though my mam and dad got divorced, I knew
how happy they had been. Since I was a young girl, I was
often talking about getting married, having kids, having
this perfect family home – I always knew it was what I
wanted.

Then, when I met Stephen, I was like, *This is it*. I just
knew from the beginning. That's probably why I pestered
him to get engaged a bit quicker, because I knew he was
the one. I think he did too, but I know what he's like.
He's stubborn. If I tell him to do something, he'll do the
opposite. If I hadn't said anything he might have proposed
earlier!

Our first dance was to 'One Day', by a band called
Kodaline, which was Stephen's choice. We used to listen
to the album all the time. It's quite slow and romantic. My
aisle song was 'A Thousand Years' by Christina Perri. I

think I made everybody cry because it's quite an emotional song, but then we did Bruno Mars on the way out, 'Marry You', which made everyone smile.

The closest I got to tears was when Dad was walking me down the aisle. I knew how much it meant to him and I knew he adored Stephen as well. As soon as he saw me in my dress he started crying – which is very rare for him. He was all right later, after he got a few beers in him.

I made sure Meat Loaf was on the DJ list because as a family we love Meat Loaf. We put some money behind the bar. It was nothing crazy, about £1,000, and we agreed that once it was gone people could buy their own drinks. At one point I went to the bar with one of my bridesmaids, who wanted to do some shots.

I still had photos to be taken as the sun went down and I was frightened to death about getting a stain on my dress. Emma ordered three Jägerbombs and they tried to charge us for them as the tab had run out. I told them to stick another £500 on. Emma was like, Steph, you can't do that. I'd had a couple and said, 'I'm the bride, I can do what I want!'

It was one of those great nights, where everybody was getting drunker and drunker, and we had bacon and sausage sandwiches and chips later on in the evening. It was some day. The wedding was at 2 p.m. and people were still going at it at 4 a.m.

The next day we booked the Worsley Marriott, near

where we lived, so instead of everybody going back home we carried it on with a big barbecue. By that afternoon, I went for a nap because I was absolutely knackered. I had to leave everybody because I was so tired, but it was a couple of days I will never forget.

THE BOY IN THE SHIRT

Things had been going really well at City and we surprised a lot of people with how quickly we progressed.

We had spent the first season training at Platt Lane with the academy and playing at the athletics stadium and then it was time to move into the brand-new City Football Academy, which had been built across the road from the Etihad.

The new complex had been a big pull in terms of going to City. You get sick of sharing grounds. You get sick of not really being the priority, having to get off the pitch if other teams wanted to play. At every club I'd been at, we had to share, and it just didn't feel like home. To actually walk in the changing rooms for the first time and play on that pitch in a pre-season friendly was just unbelievable.

I was actually quite sad to leave Platt Lane because it was so small and everybody was so together there. I have so many amazing memories. That first season was special because of everything that went on, and also how we came back from everything. We thrived on adversity. And you always go back to those moments where you're playing in the dome with those teams, playing with the likes of Phil Foden or whoever. There was a lot of firsts in that building and I was sad to leave.

But going into the new building was: wow. We'd had a tour, but obviously, until you get in there the pictures don't really do it justice. When you walk in, you're like, Oh my God, this is our own changing room. Just to have your own locker, to have a seat, to be able to say, 'This is mine.' That's huge and it was rare in women's football, even at the highest level. Rather than moving from changing room to changing room, getting shunted around, this was ours. Even the pitches that we trained on. We never got booted off! You just couldn't complain about anything. I think that was when our journey really started, when we moved into that building, and because everybody at City was moving in the same building at the same time, it felt like we all came together and started to go somewhere new.

It wasn't just the changing room and the pitches. The facilities were incredible and nothing was off limits. The first team moved to the same building, and it had everything you could think of.

We shared a treatment room, we shared the gym, we shared the ice baths. We had our own pitch. Our staff had their own office, and we learned a lot from the other staff in the building. We did a lot of learning. Having conversations with people. I like to talk to people and find out loads of stuff, so it was really good for me. The women's game has come on so much and the squad's getting so much bigger, so there's no longer enough room for us in that building and the girls are moving to a separate facility of their own, which back then would have been unthinkable. City deserve massive credit for the work they continue to pioneer in the women's game. They never stop trying to advance.

When we moved in in 2015, the men's team was on the other side of the building. But sometimes we crossed paths, and everybody was amazing. Not one person had an issue because we were the women's team. We never experienced anything like that, no sexism, no nasty comments. And we didn't put the men on a pedestal. It was always a really respectful environment, all the groups just saw each other as normal people who all worked for Manchester City.

The men's captain at the time was Vincent Kompany, and he was massive for me in terms of trying to do things together. He told me that if I ever needed anything to let him know, just anything at all. He had so much power at the club and so much influence it was great to have him in our corner. We never did really need him to help us out, but we knew that the offer was always there. To have that relationship was amazing. I wish we'd have crossed paths more often, but our schedules were very different.

With Vinny, it was all pretty normal. We got on and I remember his daughter was mascot at one of our games in that first season at the new stadium. I think it was actually one of the first times we'd played there, and he pulled me to one side and asked me if I'd mind walking out with her.

I think that was the first time I'd ever met him. We had to try and find her a kit to wear. My impression was that he was just absolutely massive and he had such a presence. I loved the way he played as a centre-half, and he was an inspiration given the way he approached playing in my position. When you listen to him and you speak to him, he has such a presence, an aura about him, and you understand why he's captain. Maybe back then, I was probably a little bit more shy than I would be now, but just even having that little conversation and being like, OK, if you need anything, just let me know, was huge. He told me just to make sure that I just kept doing me rather than putting pressure on myself. Those little reminders really go a long way when they come from someone playing right at the very top who has lifted Premier League trophies for the club. It hasn't surprised me at all that he's done so well in his managerial career and that he got the job at Bayern Munich, one of the biggest clubs in Europe, at such a young age. You could see a mile off that he was going to be a manager, and a good manager.

*

Despite the travel issues on the way back from Canada, we flew in the second half of that 2015 season and won twelve out of our last thirteen games. And the World Cup seemed to have had a big impact on the public, which we didn't really see when we were out in Canada.

We went out there and we did so well; all the City players in the squad had really good tournaments. We came back knackered, but on a massive high. For the first game after the World Cup, the stadium was packed. You see all the little girls and boys walking in and you realise the game has massively changed since the first six months.

Driving into the stadium, I saw a little boy wearing a shirt with my name on the back of it. I can't tell you how that makes you feel. I actually got emotional, sitting there in my car. I know it probably sounds really weird, but I don't know how to explain it. The whole thing that we talked about during the World Cup was to inspire the nation and make it acceptable that anybody can play football. I don't think we ever really envisaged doing what we did in the World Cup, but there was a bit of a more important message that we felt we needed to make.

Seeing that boy in a shirt with my name on the back felt crazy. It felt like a breakthrough, and not just for me. I'm sure there were other little boys going to other matches wearing shirts with the names of other England players on the back. You never, ever imagine they'll wear the name of a female footballer. You just don't think that's even a possibility. But to see a 'Houghton 5' or a 'Bronze 2' or a 'Scott 8', and to see them walking to the stadium to watch you play, was unbelievable.

I'd actually gone a different route to that game on purpose, just to see if there were bigger crowds than normal. I went the way that takes a bit longer. And, from that moment on, I always used to drive that way, up until I retired.

I'm a bit superstitious in that sense. If we had a good game or whatever, I try and drive the same way I saw the fans walk to the game. So I'd always try to drive past the Etihad, where I'd seen that little boy, because I think it kind of motivated me a little bit more.

We really were on a roll. It felt like everything was clicking and we had momentum. It was still less than two years since we'd formed but we felt like we'd moved on massively. To win so many games, we were obviously confident, but we had five or six new players that season and it takes a while for people to understand how we play, so we had a few little knocks. I missed six weeks, which was half a season, KB was injured and Jill got suspended, and we had a lot of injuries. You have a squad of eighteen and we were missing probably up to five of the starting eleven at various points throughout the season. It added a lot of pressure and a lot of challenges. But we all came back from the World Cup, and we were confident and we were fit. We wanted Champions League football. That felt like the next logical step for us. We were in a rhythm, and when you're in that moment, as a footballer, there's no one stopping you.

The manager was always asking me who I thought we could bring in. He used to ask me, Jill and Toni if there was anyone we knew of. He wanted people who were fit and who could play. Lucy Bronze and Demi Stokes, who I'd played with at Sunderland, fit the bill. Both had played a lot of international football and were technically good one-on-one defenders.

Lucy, in particular, was huge for us that season. She is also from Sunderland, and sometimes people ask me if we have something in the water up there. I don't know what it is. I actually just think we're stubborn and all have that work ethic. For all the players that I've played with from the North-East, I think, no matter what, you know what you're getting from them, whereas for some other players, maybe they're from different places where it's a flip of the coin what you're going to get: are they going to get their head down and just go?

Demi was in her last year at uni in America, and I'd mentioned to Nick that she was looking to come back home. We arranged for her to come and have a look round. She spent a few days with us, staying with me and KB. We had moved from the house that got burgled to a flat at Salford Quays, which was great, although we could see United's ground, Old Trafford, through one of the windows! Toni Duggan lived in the building as well, and Edin

Džeko from the men's team had also been there for a while. There were quite a lot of footballers in there. It was like a mini village, and a lot safer for two girls on their own than the place in Withington.

Lucy had Marie as her agent and I think some people had spotted her at the training ground, so there were conversations there. But for me, as a defender and someone that you'd want in your back four and for an England back four as well, I thought this could be the future of England's back five for a long time. So I was buzzing when they came in.

We played Notts County away in the August. It was the one game we didn't win after we came back from the World Cup, and it killed us because we drew 2–2 and ended up losing the title to Chelsea by two points.

It's funny, because it was the game that made the difference but it also sticks in my memory because I scored twice and one was one of the best goals of my career.

It was also funny because, the day before, I was practising free kicks with the assistant coach, Alan Mahon. I gave myself ten or fifteen free kicks, just trying to practise and practise and practise. They were unbelievable free kicks: I was like, Mahony, I need to stop, because I don't want to waste them all! And then I went out and scored in the game. But one thing haunts me from that. Rachel Williams did me on the counter to score for them and we just didn't see the game through. She barged through and scored in the last minute, and I think that was a bit of inexperience on our part, which was disappointing. We were gutted.

Nobody could argue, though, with the progress we had made season on season. The year before, there was only me, Jill, Toni, Izzy and KB that were really pushing in terms of what's expected. But then we had reinforcements in Lucy, whose mentality is absolutely ridiculous, and Demi, whose standards are high and who knows what you need to do in the gym, knows what to do on the pitch and in general all around. Jennifer Beattie came in as well, from Scotland and from Arsenal. We had a few more tiffs in the dressing room thanks to the type of personalities that we brought in, but ultimately the intention was to win and to push us even further. Sometimes you need to have those exchanges to get things in the open and drive improvement.

I think we also challenged the staff and the environment as a whole. And what makes it nice when it all comes together is that people were really unselfish in that period and really brought what we needed to do as a club to go and win.

It also felt like a really professional place to be. Like we were women footballers, and this was our job. It was the little things: to be able to leave your kit there, then go in the next morning and pick your kit up after it's been washed, makes a big difference. People might just think that's the norm. But for us back then, it wasn't. To have three sets of training kit, to have our own changing room, to have all our meals provided, that was a big part of being a professional, because you can focus on what you do on the pitch. The only thing that we had to worry about as players was bringing it every single day and really buying into what we were doing on the pitch, and in the gym as well. All that kind of stuff that we maybe take for granted now, back then we, as players, were like, This is crazy. I think that was what attracted people to City, as females and as footballers. To have it as easy as possible so that you can go, OK, I'm going to train. I don't have to worry about anything. I'm literally just focusing on what I'm doing on the pitch.

When you're in that environment, when you have a team that is looking after you, sorting your food, arranging your travel, it starts to shift your mindset. But I guess there is a danger of getting carried away.

It was always important to keep your feet on the ground. At times it did feel like a dream, but you had to try and put that out of your head and remind yourself that this is what we had worked hard to get and not to waste it. My mindset was that we now had an opportunity to go and win. We couldn't be going, 'Oh, well, yeah, because we only train twice a week, or we don't have food provided . . . ' They were excuses. Now we didn't have any excuses. That was when we started to get a bit more confident, because we actually had everything there to set us up to go and achieve stuff. And I think that we, as a club, but also as players, set the standard. Everybody was trying to catch up to us. We were fortunate that the timing, in terms of moving into that new facility, was unbelievable for the women's team. Arsenal had had that for a long time. Maybe not their own pitch or whatever, but they had that use of the training ground at London Colney. Whereas now we were moving into this new era, and you could see people going: 'I wonder what City's doing next?' On international camps, you'd get asked questions. People who didn't play for us had heard all about the facilities and were asking us what it was like there. And we could tell them that we got our kit done, that we went out on our own pitch. We didn't have to fight. We trained on the same schedule, every single day. To have that, and for people to ask you about it, was pretty cool, and it made the club attractive to them. If City were looking at bringing players in from other clubs, they were often pushing at an open door.

While we didn't win anything in 2015, it's hard to underestimate the impact of qualifying for the Champions League. From nothing, we had managed to gain entry to the best competition in Europe. We managed to attract players from Europe, which seemed crazy to me, given where we had come from. I think we did about ten years' work in the space of two years, which is mad. And it was always constantly changing, we were always evolving.

The problem, in a selfish sense, was that we were not the only ones. Quite a few Arsenal players went to Chelsea: you could see that momentum was kind of changing, as the manager, Emma Hayes, was starting to become a little bit more established. Emma had worked at Arsenal previously, so she had experience of what it was like as an assistant coach back then. Chelsea were also able to attract players with their facilities. I mean, Cobham is an unbelievable training ground, about twice the size of Arsenal's. You knew that they were trying to do something big. It started to feel like Chelsea were going to be our next rivals, and I hope they were thinking the same about us, because we'd only been in place for two years and we were only just getting started.

POINT PROVEN

I was shopping with my mam when Matt rang and asked me if I'd had a letter. I had no idea what he was talking about.

He then said he had something to tell me. It was all very mysterious. He said I had been nominated for an MBE in the 2016 New Year Honours List. I was like – me? Why? There had apparently been a letter, but I'd not had it. It must have gone to an old address. So the club had had a phone call from Buckingham Palace, or whoever it was, asking if I wanted this MBE! Matt said I had two hours to let them know, because I hadn't responded. Of course I wanted it, but I have to be honest: I didn't really know what it meant. Matt told me that you get those three letters after your name, and you're a Member of the Order of the British Empire. I'm not sure that has ever sunk in, because, as a kid from a mining village in the North-East, you never really associate yourself with stuff like that.

We'd met Prince William before the World Cup in 2015 and he took a massive interest in the women's game, which was amazing. But to not get the letter and nearly miss out on an MBE was pretty scary.

Matt told me I needed to try and keep it secret. Good luck with that. I told my mam, dad, brother, Stephen and his family.

You then get all the information through, and you're told the list will be released on New Year's Eve. We got a little group of us together for a meal on New Year's Eve to celebrate. We went back to Gaucho, where me and Stephen had gone on our first date, and had become a bit of a tradition when we had something to celebrate. Fara was on the list too, which was nice because she'd scored the winning goal to get us the bronze medal. I think I was chosen because I was captain. But it was all a bit surreal. We got home and me and Stephen sat up and watched Sky to see it come through on the yellow ticker, which was quite cute.

You get an invite to the ceremony and they give you a number of dates to choose from. They allow three people to go with you and I'm like, How do you choose three people to go? I've got Mam, Dad, my brother, my partner, my grandma who went everywhere. I had to request a few more, which they let me do. We went down to London the night before and stayed in a hotel near Buckingham Palace. I had to get dressed up, and they're so specific on what you can wear as a female. You have to have sleeves and your dress has to be below your knee. You've also got to wear something on your head, like a fascinator or a hat. So that was a stress in itself, working out what to wear.

When you arrive you get separated from your guests quite quickly, which doesn't help with the nerves. You are taken into a room and have half an hour before the ceremony starts to practise your curtsy and what to do when you go up.

I remember Fara being late – I was like, Fara, you can't be late for this. The only thing you should be on time for is an MBE! We practised our curtsies together.

You go out and stand in a line, and it was Princess Anne presenting the honours. She sees one person after another. I think we were standing there for about an hour and a half, and I was so nervous.

Of all the things that I've done in my career, that was probably one of the most nervous moments I've had. I loved absolutely everything about it, but it felt like it was more for my family. It was one of those days when everything's come together, and the sacrifices that they'd made to get me that MBE and have that after my name were driven home. To see so many girls who play football achieve the same thing now is amazing.

As I waited, I was thinking about where I'd come from. I'm from the North-East, and there's not many people who got MBEs from there over the years. I remember thinking that this was a dream come true. At that stage in my life, everything was just getting better and better. There weren't really many downsides. It was just fun.

So Princess Anne approaches, and you have to do the curtsy first. You walk up, you turn to face her, you curtsy, you walk, then you bow. Then you speak – you have to call her ma'am – you bow, walk back, curtsy again and walk off.

She called me Fara, and I told her I was Steph. She congratulated me and asked me how the football was going. She also told me that I did really well at the World Cup, and she knew what she was talking about.

The whole day was unbelievable because you never expect something like that will happen. Not that there wasn't a funny ending. After you get the MBE, you have to go outside and do photos and press. It's all cobbled outside the palace and my heel broke. We were going for something to eat afterwards and I was walking down the street in my dress, barefoot, like it was Sunderland town centre at two in the morning.

I was hoping it would be a successful start to a successful year. In 2015 we'd just missed out on the title and at the end of that season I gave what was one of my first major speeches. It became a thing, where at the end of the season either the manager or I would speak and assess what had happened.

I told the group that while we were disappointed not to

win the league, we should look at how far we had come, and the fact we'd got Champions League qualification was a massive step for us in two years. I was so motivated, and I wanted the pre-season to come round quickly because we finished strong and we needed to take that momentum into the new season. We needed to stay on track. We were determined to do something special that season, we really were. You could feel it within the group. I told them that while they were obviously disappointed, we all were, we could come back next season and really go for it. Again, you can't change what's happened, so the focus had to switch to the new season immediately.

We won our first game against Notts County, but we made hard work of it. We absolutely dominated them but just couldn't find a way through. In the fourth minute of injury time we got a free kick about twenty-five yards out and I tried to hit it as hard as I could. It stayed low and it went in. It felt like a huge moment. This was the type of game we'd drawn the previous season – including the one against Notts County. I think that goal banished some demons and really set us on our way.

That season we were unbelievable. Something just clicked. We felt that no matter what was thrown at us, we would find a way. We had someone that was able to score goals in Jane Ross and we were creating a lot more chances, but for me – and maybe I'm a little bit biased – defensively we were incredible. We only conceded four goals that whole season and that was not just luck: it was down to a lot of hard work. We worked so hard on the training ground and Nick was amazing in terms of technical detail. If we had questions, he always had solutions. It all came together. We didn't lose once. Out of our sixteen games, we won thirteen and drew three. We played Chelsea in the second to last game of the season and we knew if we beat them, we'd win the league with a game still to play.

We delivered the perfect performance. It was my favourite City game by far. We were dominant. There was just no way anything other than a win was going to happen. Jill headed in a corner and Toni scored a penalty, which was nice because they were two of the originals who had been there from the start.

We also kept a clean sheet against one of the top teams, who had become our main rival. I will never forget the day itself. This was what we had envisaged from the moment we all arrived. To see the stadium full, with four thousand people in there, was incredible. There was sky blue everywhere, and you know what? For once it was sunny in Manchester! The game was live on television, and it couldn't have been scripted better.

I did an interview with the BBC and, watching it back, it looks like I'm angry! I think we played that season with a bit of a chip on our shoulder. We had a point to prove. There was a lot of anti-City feeling. Some people thought we just had the most money, and it was wrong that we'd taken Doncaster's place in the league. Someone said that to me the other day, about taking Donny's place. Even ten years on it's still an issue. It wasn't me, or the girls, taking their place, it was the club. The club was doing it because they wanted to build a great women's side, and in the end it was the league who made the call.

There were a lot of doubters too. People who thought the project was going to fail. That we wouldn't make it. I don't think they really believed in us or what we had set out to do. But we proved to people that it was going to work. This is why we've come here. This is why I've moved my life from London to Manchester. This is why.

The haters just thought we had everything on a plate. They didn't see us when we used to train at Wright Robinson school when there was no room at Platt Lane. They didn't see all the work that we did at Platt Lane. They thought we were all on thousands and thousands of pounds a week. We were well paid, but it wasn't that. We weren't getting miles more than everyone else.

We'd all bought into this project and we added to the squad, but every other team in the whole of the country does that. We just wanted to make sure we improved season upon season, and we did that. We'd been in existence not even three years and we'd just gone unbeaten and won the top league in women's football in England.

When I gave that interview there was frustration because we got stick throughout those three years. You claim as a footballer you don't listen to outside noise, but you do. It's hard to ignore unless you have no phone or don't speak to anyone in the world. And even then, every time you came into our building Sky Sports was on. Social media was growing, so you could see what people were saying. But there was a real togetherness about that group. We knew what we needed to do, and we never got big-headed or ahead of ourselves. We shut a lot of people up. We just ticked each game off as we went along, but there was real intent to try and pick up that trophy. And I just love the fact that we did it by playing the way we wanted to play. We played with a philosophy that we worked so hard on. It was all about being in control. Control the ball as much as you possibly can and recognise where the space is. Try and get forward as much as possible, which sometimes takes a little bit of patience until you can pick the right pass. Defensively, make sure you are hard to beat. We were so aggressive in our press, we were so fit as a team and we were so agile that no matter what any team threw at us, we were able to come up with solutions. That was probably the most pleasing thing for the manager. Even though he gave us guidance, we had players on the pitch that could solve problems straight away.

When we started in 2014, Nick had told us that we were going to be successful but that we were also going to change the perception of women's football, the perception that it wasn't as important as male football and that females didn't really have an opportunity or a chance of playing at that level. I feel as though, slowly but surely, we did change that. We knew that we were going to try and play exactly the same way as the men. We were going to do exactly the same as the men in terms of how we prepared, what we did, how were seen from the outside.

It takes time to change people's opinions and how they think about you. But because we were successful and seen as hardworking and motivated and wanting to win, people accepted it. They accepted that it was only right that females play and can chase their dreams. A lot of men were involved, and I think that also helps. It's not just a female staff. It's not them and us. And the female and male staff were determined to break down barriers.

We would hear it a million times: if the best men's team played the best women's team they would thrash them. Well, obviously they would, because from a physical point of view of course men are stronger and faster.

Before tournaments under Hope Powell we always used to play against lads' teams, and we always used to get beaten. But it was about the physical outcome, more of a fitness thing, for us. If we could get the ball, it'd be about making better decisions because it was tough to get it back.

But that men are automatically better is just a lazy assumption, if I'm being honest. It's stupid and it's not only ignorant, it's wrong. A few weeks ago I did my coaching course at St George's Park. There were ten women and three men playing, and the lads had all played League Two football.

We had to do a little drill together. Technically I was probably better than the three lads, and this is not me being big-headed, it was just how it was. But they were faster than me and stronger than me. The differences are mainly from a physical point of view. Of course they can hit the ball a bit harder just because they're stronger, but in terms of passing and knowledge of the game, I don't think there's that much difference, especially at the higher level.

It frustrates me when people just dismiss the women's game, because more often than not they've never even been in and around what we do on a day-to-day basis. I'd say come and actually sit down and speak to us if you want to really know what that's about, because we work so hard to be at the top level within our sport. I watch football all the time and if anybody wants a tactical conversation, I'll have it.

I see a lot of female pundits get incredible stick, especially online. Look, it doesn't matter if it's me or you speaking. I'd be confident enough to have that kind of argument and I can be on that level. Maybe if the top WSL team played against a League Two side they would get battered. Maybe they wouldn't. But even if they did, it doesn't change the talent we have in the game or what we've done to get to this point.

I'd ask people to stop trying to compare it, because men aren't playing women's football. This is a separate sport. And we need to almost forget the men's game when we're talking about the women's game. Just focus on women's football like you do with women's tennis, for example. No one's saying, 'Oh, well, you know, Roger Federer would smash the best women' because it's a different game.

A lot of these people making that judgement have probably never played a game of football in their life. And I'm like, How can you? You've not even been a part of it. So I think that's what I mean by lazy. I'm like, You've not really taken the time to get to know us. At City we have the same concepts as Pep does for his first team. And if you actually watched what City did, or if somebody did something using AI where they took the heads off the players and they showed how two different goals were created, I don't think you could tell whether it was the men's team or the women's team.

It's frustrating that people still say these things, but I do feel as though we are challenging that quite a lot more now, and the 2016 season was a big part of that.

There are also people who try and use women's football to get themselves on the news with some random comment. Some of these people have wives and daughters, and it blows my mind that they speak about women the way they do.

These are women who have had very good careers in

the game. Lucy Ward has often been a target. For me she's probably one of the best commentators, but I think some people don't actually listen. They just hear a female voice and get wound up; their judgement gets clouded by the fact it's a woman talking.

I hope it gets to a stage where this isn't an issue, but I'm doubtful. I don't want to be derogatory, but I think some just get jealous that women are able to play at the top of the game but they never had that chance. When people say women get jobs in commentary as part of a box-ticking exercise, it annoys me. It's not like that. You actually look at what they've achieved in football and what they know about it, and it's just the same as any male pundits or players.

The game's the game. It's a ball, it's two goals, it's the same-sized pitch. It's eleven players on each team. We all watch football; we all have an opinion on football. We've all either played or we've been a part of it.

A comment was made recently about tackles, about how being tackled by a men's player is different. Of course it might be more forceful, but I played against players like Katie Chapman, and you wouldn't want to get tackled by her because she would tackle and she would tackle hard. It might be seen as a different thing, but it's the same action. It's the same pass or same defender move, same header or clearance. It's all the same things.

'DO WHAT YOU NEED TO DO'

One afternoon before we got married, Stephen came home from training and I could tell from the look on his face that there was something wrong.

'Steph,' he said. 'My hand just slipped off the steering wheel when I was driving.' I didn't know what he meant so I asked him if he had pins and needles or something. He said he didn't, his hand had just slipped off. I thought it was weird but really didn't think much else. I just said we'd keep an eye on it.

The weeks and months went on and he kept saying that he felt a little bit weak in his right-hand side when he was at the gym. And because Stephen is quite slight, he had to work hard on his gym. He wouldn't miss a set, he wouldn't miss a rep. He would be so hard working, and he'd do everything he was told to do. He said he felt like his pull-ups were getting harder, and he kept repeating that he just felt a bit weaker.

I started to notice a bit of twitching in his tricep. It was random at first but then it started to become continuous. At this stage I told him he was going to have to go and speak to the doctor and the physio, and find out what was going on.

He did that and they both said that they'd keep an eye on it. Stephen and the Bradford physio went to a neurologist in Leeds, where he had tests on his neck, his arms, his nerves – any tests that you can imagine, he started to have.

They didn't really have any idea what was going on and, looking back, that was one of the hardest parts, the fact that we didn't know. But at the time he was still playing football, still training every single day, still working hard.

But I could see he was finding it a bit harder to be motivated for football, and that wasn't Stephen. I can't say enough that wasn't him. At the time he was on the bench at Bradford, he'd been stripped of the captaincy and a new manager, Stuart McCall, had come in. Things were changing at the club, and I wondered if he was feeling that way because he wasn't playing as much and because he wasn't captain any more. I raised that with him, but he was adamant that wasn't the reason.

You could tell it was all playing on his mind. As time went by, he just didn't feel right. He was then referred to a professor of neurology in Sheffield called Chris McDermott. He wanted to do some more tests.

Professor McDermott was a neurological specialist; he

was one of the best in the country. He called for EMG tests and nerve conduction studies. And Stephen had a lumbar puncture. He also had a week in hospital receiving immunoglobulin infusions, which meant he missed two Bradford games.

There were lots of appointments as we tried to find out what was wrong and sometimes I wasn't able to go with him so he'd be there with his mum and dad. All the way through he'd be telling me that everything was going to be OK and that there was nothing to worry about, that he'd get sorted. I felt so guilty for not being there. A lot of the time it was because I was away with England.

At that stage I didn't have a clue what was going on because everything was still pretty normal. He was playing football and going out with the lads, and we were planning our wedding. His contract ran out at Bradford, and his old manager, Phil Parkinson, had gone to Bolton and wanted to take him there. I remember we went to the women's Champions League final in Cardiff and Stephen came with us, and Matt at the time was trying to sort his deal out. To get it done, they needed his medical records. There was a question mark about what was going on, because his twitches were getting a little bit worse. Around that time the doctor told us it was 90 per cent not something called motor neurone disease. That was the first time anyone had mentioned MND.

Stephen passed his medical, signed for Bolton and we

got married. Life was pretty much still normal, so in my eyes nothing was changing. But when I think back to our wedding I often think about Stephen and how emotional he was. He obviously didn't feel great. He'd been wanting us to get married for a long time, and he loves his family and mine, so it was the perfect day in that sense. But there was definitely a bit of a cloud hanging over him. I don't want to put words in his mouth, but I think I understand.

That summer, Stephen said he didn't know if he could physically play any more. I just couldn't understand why he wouldn't want to play. He was at a big club at Bolton. He'd got the support. He'd got a manager that he really liked, and he absolutely loved the assistant manager, Steve Parkin.

But he told me he just didn't feel right when he was training, he didn't feel strong enough. So then me and his dad suggested that maybe he needed to just do a bit more in the gym and maybe get more physio, get some extra help to help him get better.

He told us he couldn't hold people off any more when he was playing. And obviously, because of his size, playing in that league he needed to be able to use his body against the best wingers.

We didn't clash, but we had differences of opinion on what the next step should be.

Stephen put his head down and went back to football, but I think his mindset was that it was a job, whereas before he still probably saw it as a hobby that he loved. He'd come back in from training and he wouldn't really talk about it, he'd just say it was OK.

So we went back to Professor McDermott and he said that they needed to rule out MND. Ever since then I've fucking hated going across Snake Pass to Sheffield. On the way home, I googled MND on my phone because I had no idea what it was. I opened the first page and just closed it straight away. Stephen was in the front with his dad and I was in the back. I knew I needed to be normal for him. That page I looked at, it jumped out at me that the life expectancy is awful. Two years. I didn't want to see that.

Stephen then had another appointment in September, but I wanted him to change it because we were playing Atletico Madrid away in the Champions League. He told me I didn't need to come, that it was going to be absolutely fine. So I flew to Spain. We got there around lunchtime and I knew Stephen's appointment was two in the afternoon, English time. So I had three hours. I'd asked him if he was sure he didn't want me to be there because I could have got a later flight after the appointment. City wouldn't have minded me missing training the night before the game. They were great with stuff like that. But he was adamant. We do normal, he said. It's your work – you need to go. That was a big thing with us, keeping things normal.

For example, if I had something on and I wanted him to come, but he had training the next day he wouldn't come.

We sacrificed time together because we were so conscious that we wanted to do what's right for work and for football and for ourselves, really. That's how we've always worked. We missed out on a lot of things in the early years, but it worked because we were both happy in that sense, that we knew we were doing the right thing.

I was like, OK, fine, as long as your mum and dad go with you – I don't want you going by yourself. So his mum and dad went, and I think Matt was there as well, to support Stephen every step of the way.

Stephen had been around the squads at Bolton, he'd been in and out. But whereas he'd have been furious to be left out at Bradford, he wasn't too fussed which worried me.

They went to the appointment, and I was checking my phone all the time. It seemed to take ages. The appointments we'd been to were pretty short and sharp, about fifteen minutes, but this had been half an hour and I'd not heard anything.

It got to 4 p.m. back home and I'd still not heard from Stephen. I began to think something was wrong. You just get a feeling. This wasn't right.

Finally Matt phoned, and asked if there was somewhere I could go by myself. Then Gav Makel, the City general manager, asked me to come with him. I was like, What the fuck's going on? Why do people want me to be by myself? Jennifer Beattie came with me, and we sat near the lobby, where the hotel reception was.

You know what? I can't remember the phone call that came next. All I can remember is Ste asking me if I was OK. I asked him what the matter was, what he'd been told. He said, 'Yeah, I've got MND.' I asked him if he was joking. I actually thought he was joking. I don't know what we said in the rest of the conversation. All I could think was that I needed to get home. My head was a mess, wondering what it meant. By the time we were having this conversation the manager had come over and Gav was there too. Beatts was with me and a girl called Becs, who was a player liaison, joined us.

I was just crying my eyes out. They told me they'd got my flight home sorted, so they obviously knew.

I don't know how to say what I felt. I think my first thought was that he was there by himself, even though he was with his mum and dad, and that I should have been with him. So I felt guilty.

Then I was thinking, What does that mean for us as a couple? Stephen was twenty-nine. We'd just got married. Has this really happened? And then I thought, Right, OK, I need to get on the flight. It was going in an hour and a half. I went and got my bag, and the team psychologist came with me. She was called Lorraine, and she was amazing. She came all the way back to Manchester with me. We had a flight to London then had to get a car back, because there was no direct flight.

That journey was the longest you could ever imagine.

To know what had happened was just awful, and I didn't really know what the future would hold in terms of us as a couple.

I was worried about Stephen. What does this mean? I was just seeing him as my husband. I was not seeing him as anybody else, or someone that had got a disease. What does it mean for his football? What's he going to do? We landed at about six and then it was three and a half hours home. Physically I may have been there on the way home, but mentally I was gone. I was constantly texting, seeing if he was OK. I know it took him a while to tell me over the phone, it was just the hardest way to tell me. I still feel guilty to this day for not being there. He was texting me back, telling me it will be fine. He just stayed positive because that's how he is and I was thinking, How can you even be like that while this is happening?

I remembered what I'd seen about MND on the way back from Sheffield that time, but I still didn't really know what MND was. Normally, with any other thing, I'd be head-on, solving problems, trying to figure it out, but not now.

All I did in the car was try to watch some shit TV pro-gramme that I'd saved on my phone, just to try to keep my mind off it, because how do you manage when you've had that news?

I got back home and his mum and dad were at the house. His brother had been working and he didn't go to the appointment either, so he had come over and they were all waiting for me to get back.

I saw Stephen and I just gave him a hug. I don't know what we said. I still can't remember to this day. If I asked him, he wouldn't know either. And he probably didn't need me to say anything. Maybe not until the next day. I don't think we went to bed until about four or five in the morning, and we didn't say much to each other. We were just hugging.

When we got up, my first thought was that I was going to retire from football. I just couldn't process it all. I knew we had another appointment on Monday to ask questions. Stephen was already thinking when to announce his retirement. Get the news out straight away. And I asked if we needed to do it so quickly. But he was adamant that that was how he wanted to deal with the whole thing. Meanwhile, I was thinking, What does this mean for us as a couple? What does this mean for him? How is he going to cope? What does this mean for the future? What does this mean for my football? What does this mean for everything? So many questions and there were just no answers.

I asked if they'd told him what he could do. Whether there was any medication. What happens now. And he said we just wait.

I couldn't get my head around that. I was like, 'What do you mean, we just fucking wait?' He told me they couldn't do anything, which I just couldn't understand or accept. We live in this developed world, with so much going on, we've moved on so much and you're telling me there's nothing they can do? But that's how it is. With MND, they can't do anything. It blew my mind, and it still does. That's the most frustrating thing about the whole disease – there's no cure. There's no 'If you do this, you'll get better'. There's nothing like that. And that was probably the hardest thing about it, that there was nothing that we could do to help.

We were like, OK, nutrition-wise, what can we do? There's not much research on that. Exercise-wise, rehab-wise, what can we do? There's not much research on that. And I thought, Surely, come on, any injury, anything, any illness, there's always a tablet or there's a rehab programme. Because we're sportspeople as well, you always think, What can we do better? Especially because we've been in so many amazing clubs and had so many resources, more than anybody else with that condition.

But there was nothing that I could say and nothing that I could do, nothing that we could prepare. Nothing I could organise was ever going to help, because there was nothing to help at that time.

We went to Worsley the morning after, and we got a coffee and started walking along the canal. Ste's attitude was, Look, everything stays the same, we don't change. We still do what we do. I know football's going to change and my life's going to change a little bit, but we still do what we've done all the time. We still see our families, we still go out, we see our friends. The hardest part was that he was so amazing. I think I would have been reacting in a different way. I'd be so angry. I'd be like, Why us? We've just got married. We've got everything ahead of us. We're in a good position financially. We were looking forward to having kids. We'd bought a house. We'd done the house out. Everything was going for us. Everything. But then you get that news and the world turns upside down.

Stephen told me he wanted me to go back to football the next day. I said I couldn't leave him, but he insisted.

He said, no matter what, you do what you need to do. I told him, Look what happened when I left you the last time. But he said the way I would cope would be by just throwing myself back into football.

I think back now to that week, and it was just surreal. Within seven days we'd announced it on all the news channels. We put out a statement saying that Stephen had MND. I remember it was on the yellow ticker on Sky. People started to message us and it all became a bit over-whelming. So, from the day of him being diagnosed to maybe seven days later, he'd retired and it was all out there.

Life was going to change but for Stephen, in his head, that was probably the right thing to do. Now when I reflect back I feel as though we should have maybe taken a couple of months and just processed it as a family. For me, my out was going to football. But it didn't hide what we were going through at home. I could switch off for two hours, but as soon as I finished and was off the pitch, it was like, OK, I want to get back home now.

Everything in those seven short days just changed dramatically.

HOPE

We always had a plan. Euro 2021 would be my final tournament. I'd retire at City and Stephen would carry on playing. We'd have kids and I'd stay at home with the babies.

But that was all gone. We had different priorities now. When you get diagnosed with MND, there are things you need to do.

We were advised to bank Stephen's voice for when the time comes that he can't use it, and to put things in place if we wanted to have kids in the future.

All these things were thrown at us within the space of a couple of months. We did it so quickly, which was the best thing we could have done because I know that people have waited and missed those opportunities, and you really don't know what kind of progression the disease is going to have.

The length of time between Stephen's symptoms and his diagnosis suggested that it would progress relatively slowly.

The first twitch and diagnosis were eighteen months apart and not a lot had changed in that time, so the impression was that it wasn't going to be quick, which has been proven to be right.

If you're looking for positives, some people don't get that because it hits so quickly. You could say that we were lucky in that sense.

Nick picked me for the next game, but he asked me if I was OK first and told me to do what I needed to do. He said, whatever happens, when I came back in I'd be playing, I'd be captain. The club, from the beginning right through to now, have been unbelievable and I know that they would do the same for anybody.

Without the support of my friends at City, it would have been impossible. For those first three or four months, I never missed training. I never missed one session.

I don't actually know how I managed that year. I think my motivation was Stephen. We went to Bristol away and I don't think I ever stopped running because I was like, I can still play football, I still have that opportunity, but Stephen's just retired. He can't do this. So I'm so fucking lucky that I can do what I do still, and I'm doing it for both of us now. That was my mindset as the season went on: it's not just me now, it's for him.

I also wondered what he would be like if it was the other way round. I know he would be exactly the same. My perspective started to change a little bit in that sense. Football was always a priority, but if anything was to happen with family, that would come first regardless.

That's not to say I didn't question why it had happened. That thought kept going around my head. Why us?

The chances of getting MND are about one in three hundred people or something stupid like that. Nobody else in the family has had it.

I was just thinking about all kinds of things, like did he bang his head when he was younger? But the worst thing we could have done was felt sorry for ourselves. And I think we knew that. We knew that if that was our state of mind, the MND was going to progress quicker. A lot of your strength comes from your mentality. If you get that right, you can achieve more and you can stay stronger. We relied on each other quite a lot, and we have amazing families as well. It really helped that they were there in that first week to ten days. We had a lot of people coming to the house to see us, which was amazing. And, you know, so many negative things are said about football, but in that moment, football showed what it's about, that it can be incredibly positive. It's not just about money and people's egos, it's about putting the person first. That was so evident in the support of Bolton, Bradford and Liverpool, who have all been unbelievable with Stephen because he's one of their own. It was just really overwhelming, to be honest.

*

Stephen was introduced to a man called Chris Rimmer through his brother Kevin. Chris had been diagnosed with MND two years before Stephen. They got talking, and that was the best thing ever, for Stephen to speak to someone with the disease and find out as much about the disease as possible. He then started to delve into more research and what he could do with his diet. Chris helped him massively in terms of trying to keep positive and to really think, OK, what can we actually control? With MND, because of how it affects the nerves in your brain and spinal cord, you're burning shitloads of calories. Your body's working so hard because you're twitching all the time. Stephen naturally lost weight quite easily when he was playing football, so it was massively important for us to try and make sure he was eating good things. Obviously, there would be off days, and it's OK to have chocolate, but the balance was important. As well as what he could do with his diet, Stephen focused on whether he could start doing physio and try to keep the strength up in his legs, because you can't just go from professional football to doing absolutely nothing.

I didn't want to smother him with more information. Of course, I had conversations on the side and asked doctors at City and England if they knew any neurologists that we could speak to. But I just thought, I need to be a wife now.

I don't need to be someone that's telling him stuff all the time. I want us to be husband and wife still. And I can be that person that is as normal as possible for him. He can speak to Chris, and he can speak to other people about MND. I don't want our life to be ruined by MND, dominated by MND. And he wanted me to be that person. I would never come in and say, 'Stephen, have you seen this article? This research?' That wasn't my way of coping. If I had done that, I don't think I would be where I am today or have really done what I have over the last few years. My thing was to just be a wife, make jokes, look after him to a point, let him be what he wants to be, because he was very independent anyway, and allow him to have his freedom as much as possible. That's the way that we decided to work.

It's been six years now since diagnosis, and from a physical point of view it's harder for Stephen. He's quite dependent on me, and his mum and dad, who retired to help us. He's using the walker now and also in a wheelchair. If he wants to go out or go get some fresh air, he's in the chair. In the mornings, I help him get ready and prepare his meals. He is very dependent on other people, which is not nice, but at the same time, from a mental point of view, a positivity point of view, he's stronger than ever, which is amazing.

I think the last two years have been tougher than the other four because he was able to do things by himself, he was able to drive, he was able to go to see his mates, he was able to cook his own tea, do his smoothies. Whatever he wanted, he had his independence. Whereas now we have to arrange our whole life around who can be there for Stephen when I'm working, when I'm at football. Even stuff like going on holiday, we have to make different arrangements to make sure we can get assistance.

It's really hard for him that he can't live the life that he should be living. But I think we make it work: we still have a laugh, we're still able to see our nephews, we're still able to do stuff, and we don't stop going anywhere because of it. One thing we said was that we wouldn't just sit in the house and do nothing. We still go out, we still see people, and if it makes it easier, people come and see us at the house. We adapt, really. We just adapt with everything that we do.

Stephen can still communicate so we're not using the voicebank yet. Fingers crossed we don't have to use it. But it's becoming harder for him to speak because the muscles in his neck and in his throat are not as strong as they used to be. I can always tell when he's been chatting to the family, because when I come in he's a bit tired. I'll say, 'You've been talking all day, haven't you?' But sometimes he's quiet and it's not because he doesn't want to talk, he is just resting his voice. I understand what he's saying, but if people have been away from us for a few weeks and come back, it can be quite hard for them to understand. But he's still able to communicate with us and he still has a sense of humour. He's still taking the mick out of me all the time!

There are still good days at the moment. I usually have to help him get up the stairs, but the other day he flew up, which was amazing. Something to celebrate. And I think I'm very conscious to let him know when he's been amazing at doing the simple things we take for granted.

He knows when he's finding it harder to get up the stairs, but when he's in a normal walk and rhythm, I make sure I tell him that that's good. Even the little things like him being able to get up off his seat.

We haven't made that many adaptations to the house so not much has changed, which is good, but he's got his own recliner chair to help him relax a little bit more. And he chose this big black chair. I was like, 'Stephen, the whole house is grey. Why don't you pick a grey chair?' It's important that I'm like that with him, because it's us being a couple.

We're in a good place, because at the moment we have so many more good days than bad ones. It helps that we have his mum and dad, who are so positive, and they couldn't be any more understanding of the situation. His brother, who probably knows him best, comes over and is really calm with him, and it's nice for him to have conversations with different people, rather than just me.

I've felt so guilty sometimes, when I've come in and moaned about football, but he wants me to be like that. That's just how it should be. We're in it together no matter what. And he's still unbelievable at giving advice as well. I don't know where he gets that from. The number of people who say he's just absolutely amazing, and I'm like, I know.

They can't get their heads around the positivity, and ask if he's like that all the time. And he is.

He set up the Darby Rimmer Foundation with Chris, and part of that was to help others, because when you have that meeting with a neurologist and they give you the diagnosis, there's not much help or support. It's a very lonely place to be. Chris was there to support Stephen. Without their conversation over the first two or three months, that guidance and support from someone who knows what he's going through, I don't know where Stephen would be.

It also helped massively that he was given a purpose, doing what they did with the foundation. And that's not just a Stephen thing. A lot of footballers struggle when they retire.

Stephen had been at Liverpool from the age of eight and his life ever since then revolved around football. Day to day was always football, so when that stops, what do you do?

Even now, when I get home he's been on the computer all day, doing emails. He still has that work ethic and the desire to help and support people. The foundation has helped so many people, and it's raised £2.1 million.

Sometimes I tell him that he needs to stop doing so much work, that he needs to relax and chill more. But it gives him the drive every single day, to do something and to be involved in something. Now I'm retired I think I understand it a little better, because I have days now where I wonder what I am supposed to do with myself.

*

This all sounds positive, but it's not always like that. There are dark days and it's not nice to see him struggle. But he's so stubborn and independent, sometimes he feels like I am smothering him. I'll offer help and he'll say no. It's very hard to see someone you love be in that state and for them to refuse your help. He's not in pain, but it's hard because he's so weak.

When he is in that state and he doesn't want my help, it's hard for us both to stay positive.

There have also been days that have been difficult for different reasons. But I think in those dark days, it is so important that we make a conscious effort to get our nephews over as much as possible. Stephen's brother's boys, Thomas and James, who are seven and four. They're at an age where they're just so cheeky, they're absolutely amazing. They're just so happy, coming over to play on their Nintendos, play footy in the garden, fighting, because they're into the fighting stage now.

Sometimes when it's a dark day I ask Kev if he can bring the boys over, or if we come and see them. Having different people around allows you to not think about the situation for a while.

A change of scenery is another way of dealing with it. Sometimes we go to the cinema, to just get out the house and not be reminded by the recliner chair or think about the fact that we need to be eating every two or three hours.

Stephen can't drive any more. You actually have to send

your licence back to the DVLA. What's that all about? Can you imagine having to do that? It's just not normal, and it's not very nice. Stephen did it himself. He went to an appointment, and he told them that he didn't feel as though he was strong enough to drive. The insurance had already gone sky high, and he just said it wasn't worth the risk. By that time, his mum had retired, so we knew that there would always be somebody there to drive him if we needed. We knew there were ways and means, but it just kind of breaks your heart a little bit.

Stephen is from a Catholic family, and I think he and his mum went to church a little bit more after the diagnosis. I know his mum started to go a little bit more frequently. It can be hard for me to understand that, because I'm not Catholic.

If you start to beat yourself up about why this has happened, how God could let this happen, you're just wasting so much energy. We need as much energy as we can, and if going to church helps, then we'll take it. It's not as if you're going to stop believing in what you believe in because of this. I couldn't even think what he's thinking about, to be honest. I wouldn't even want to ask him.

When it comes to the future, it probably sounds hard to believe but it isn't something we have spoken about much. We don't look that far ahead. Before we got married, before the diagnosis, I had that Euro 2021 plan. Retire, have kids.

I thought Stephen could play for as long as he wanted because he was so fit. But now we just take each year as it comes. Let's go with how we're feeling and how we are, and we adapt from there.

We do still want kids. That will happen whenever it happens, but we want it to be as soon as possible. That's the idea. We always wanted to be quite young parents. We want Thomas and James to have a little cousin. We still talk positively about it, and we know it would be different, me and Stephen having a kid. It would be a lot harder than for other parents. We would need a lot of help, but we need a lot of help now, so it might not make too much of a difference.

It's important that we speak positively about the future, rather than negatively. We've never put a time frame on anything. If we start thinking that we might have only x number of years, we're beaten already. And we don't want it to ever be like that.

We honestly don't think like that. We don't think about life expectancy. When you do it means that MND has beaten us all. Things may change. Manchester's our home now, but we might move closer to Ste's mum and dad in Liverpool, especially if we have kids, because we want them to go to the same school as Thomas and James.

We have hope for the future, which is the only way we get through. I would hate for us to plan for the worst, because you just end up thinking about that for all of the years to come and those times are precious. From all my experience and chats I have had with the families of people who have MND, the moment you start thinking like that things deteriorate quickly. I would never want it to be like that for Stephen or for our families either.

We still hold massive hope of a miracle outcome.

Especially over the past few years, because of the amount of money that we've raised as a foundation as much as anything else: £2.1 million is unbelievable for a charity that really only has Stephen and Matt running it. It's a small charity and nobody gets paid to do it. The success is down to a lot of different people. Rob Burrow and Kevin Sinfield have been amazing. Marcus and Louise Stewart, Ed Slater, Doddie Weir. Doddie was massive for Stephen. He launched his foundation first and he was such an inspirational person in how he dealt with everything and what he achieved, along with Rob. We loved them both so much.

There's a lot more positive research going on now than there was when Stephen was diagnosed, which is due to the money that's been invested. But there's not enough money going into MND for how many people it affects in the country. It's actually ridiculous. It might only be one in three hundred, but if you think about your average school that's three kids, three kids at every school who will get it. That's the most frustrating thing. For any other disease, there's so much money and research in finding cures. But why not this? It's just massively underfunded. And I don't actually know why.

That was why Stephen wanted to set up the foundation. He could have control of where the research money goes. There's an MND community now, and everyone works together to raise as much awareness as possible.

I still think there could be a major development in the next few years.

I still hope.

GETTING PAID

The 2017 season was a weird one because we were switching from summer to winter and only played eight games. I felt like we were just going through the motions after the highs of the season before. We drew with Liverpool on each side of the break, which was enough to make sure we didn't retain the title.

But we did win the FA Cup and I got to lift a trophy at Wembley for the first time. We were playing Birmingham, who'd had a really good season, but we were confident. We'd added Carli Lloyd, who was a mega signing for us. The Americans had always set the benchmark in the women's game and I learned so much. She wasn't at City for long, but I got an insight into how she'd won everything that she had.

I learned so much from her mentality. She has a big American, driven personality and could come across as selfish initially and I wondered how she would fit in, but everything she did was aimed at making the team better.

When anyone joined, we always used to do physical testing. One of the tests was jumping. Carli didn't score too highly but she wasn't embarrassed. She just said, 'If you put the ball up there, I'll win it!' She meant business. She was also the first player I would see going out after we'd trained to do shooting practice.

Lucy Bronze scored the first goal in that final. She took it right off my head! We ended up winning 4–1 and I got to walk up those steps for the first time. I can remember there were loads of them – it must have been over a hundred.

The best thing was that you walk past your family. Just to get that trophy and to do what so many amazing people have done, men's and women's captains and teams, in that same spot was unbelievable.

I'll never forget the celebrations either, not least because I didn't cut my heel this time! We all stayed at the Hilton next to the stadium. We got everybody's families, all the girls, all the staff back there, and it was literally just music and alcohol. The sports scientists brought in our cooler box, and it was full of booze. I don't think you would be able to get away with doing that now.

We got knocked out of the Champions League by Lyon in the semi-finals that year. The damage was done in Manchester when they won 3–1, but we beat them at their place 1–0 in the second leg. It wasn't enough, but Carli scored, and it was the first time they'd lost in a long, long time. There were around twenty thousand there, which was a reminder that we still had a lot of work to do in our own country. Our league was getting stronger, but it wasn't at the level it is now. It was all quite a new experience for everybody. You'd go there and play against a team with a very hostile crowd. The Champions League crowd was very different.

In the next few seasons, we just couldn't manage to get over the line. There aren't many matches in the league so if you lost against one of your rivals early on it was pretty much game over. That's why the league needs more strong teams, to retain the interest.

That season Lyon knocked us out of the Champions League again, and you start to ask questions. Is it the way that we play, is it the tactics? Is it the personnel? Do we need more players? Is it me personally, what could I do differently? Every player in Lyon's squad was a full international, and the best in their national team, whether that was France or somewhere else. Lucy went to play for them because she wanted to win the Champions League. Sadly, they never came in for me! Joking aside, if they had, I would have had a decision to make. PSG came in a few times and there were other approaches, but I always felt a loyalty to City, not a lack of ambition. I was playing every single week, and playing for England; I was competing for trophies and I was happy.

Financially, too, things had started to change for the better. I signed new contracts and each was an increase on the last one. The money was going up substantially as the game got bigger. I had been on around £7,000 with Arsenal and my first City contract was £24,000. The next year it went up to £40,000 and carried on rising.

The commercial side started to take off, going to around £70–80,000 a year. Being England captain, I did an ad for Virgin Media. Nike also came on board, then Lucozade and Cadbury's.

Matt was instrumental in the talks. England men's and women's players were doing commercial appearances, and the men were getting £38,000 for two hours while the women got £5,000. No matter how you dressed that up, it was wrong. We were all in a Head and Shoulders ad, and we got £5,000 while the men got £40,000 – and we actually did more than them in the ad! That ad was crazy. The compromise to the £5,000 was that I would be flown down after training in the helicopter Kyle Walker would be coming back in. That was the only way I could make it work and get there on time. But it was important to take these opportunities when we were offered them, given where we had come from.

To be fair, some of the senior men's players, like James Milner and Jordan Henderson, told the FA to put the money in a pot and split it equally. But the FA thought the other men might have had an issue. There was this feeling that they couldn't upset the male players, when the reality was that they were probably more on board than the execs who were making the decisions.

There were also the differences with things like transport. A couple of years ago, the PFA held a big meeting in Manchester about player scheduling. Gianni Infantino, the FIFA boss, was there, and Arsène Wenger. Some really big names. Player-wise there was Harry Maguire, Paul Pogba, Conor Coady. At the end of it Fernandinho, who was the City men's captain at the time, came over. He'd found out that while they flew to matches in places like Brighton, we had to get the bus.

Fernandinho was great. He said, Whatever we do, we do the same. He didn't have to come and say that. But they started to know from that conversation that they were flying to Brighton and that's just a normal thing for them. We get a five-hour bus journey to Brighton and they're complaining about the schedule.

But it still rankled. Pogba was complaining about the fact that he had to take a half-an-hour flight to Newcastle to play St James's Park. So I pointed out that we had to go to London on a bus, then we had to play Champions League or a midweek game two days later and nobody complained.

Playing for England has come on a long way and the FA eventually addressed the issues, but it took a long time to persuade them.

It's very different now from when I was captain. You'd always get the same people doing a lot of things. We wanted to try and help make it fair. Brands would always pick certain players, which is understandable. But now players just get paid a certain rate every single camp, which basically covers your central contract, and the girls do commercial afternoons in camp. You get around £10–16,000 and everybody has a turn.

Tournament bonuses for the Lionesses have shot up, which was a long time coming and it is only right because the prize money has also gone up.

I probably didn't reap the rewards that future generations will, but it was a ten-year battle. People like me and Lucy fought over every small detail with the FA. It was challenging and there were a lot of setbacks, but we kept at it. Sometimes it was painful just to get the smallest margins. When I started, we'd have the conversations with the manager, but that changed and by the end it was with Mark Bullingham, the head of commercial, who went on to become chief executive of the FA.

We had a leadership group: Casey Stoney was in there, Jordan Nobbs, Laura Bassett. Lucy would come in. It would rotate, but I was a mainstay. I used to just put it out there, what we wanted and why I thought it was justified. Lucy was always at the front too.

At one stage we went on strike. That's how bad it was. It ended up getting leaked to one of the newspapers and the FA suddenly changed their whole stance. I think that was the first time we realised we had power. Power in striking and power in using the media. We stuck together as a squad throughout, even though there were sometimes hard conversations to be had.

When you've come from nothing and you don't expect anything, to go into meetings with people that are very experienced is a difficult job. The FA had so much control over our money and income, and maybe until you get older you actually don't know the ins and outs of how it works. Matt was really important in terms of letting us know that we had value. And it was important that we approached it in a way that was really humble, but logical.

We couldn't just go, 'Just fucking give us more money', even though it was really tempting to do that because it was ridiculous what the lads were getting compared to us. But it was important to have humility when we were trying to push boundaries.

Matt was surprised at how little we knew. For example, we might get 10 per cent of the prize money when in reality that should be 50–60 per cent, minus costs and everything else. We had been happy with our 10 per cent, but when we started to get educated and feel our own worth we became a lot more powerful.

A lot of the information was accessible. The prize money is on the internet! And to be fair to the team, they trusted me a lot. For the leadership group, it was always important to update the girls when we had conversations. The girls are not very good at texting back, or you'd make a group or whatever but it wouldn't work. I was always conscious that I didn't want them to think that we were having conversations behind their back. Though I have to admit, sometimes we did. We had to, because we wouldn't get stuff done otherwise. It's impossible to get thirty players, who are all on different schedules, in different locations, together for a meeting. And the FA wouldn't let us do it in camp. There was just no way that would happen. So we had to be quite clever about it.

In 2015, not everyone knew that we could get a World Cup bonus. We beat Norway in the round of sixteen, and it was the first time we had ever got past that stage. I can't remember who it was, but someone was like, 'Get in, we get a bigger bonus!' Honestly, some didn't realise. But that's life-changing money for some people, it's a big part of a deposit on a house. Fortunately, it's moved on massively since then.

And it wasn't just what we got paid. The contracts were ludicrously one-sided. The termination processes were terrible. There were so many different elements of the contract that it was 98 per cent the FA and 2 per cent the players. But the players felt like they were privileged to have a contract at all, and so they just took the money.

When you start getting professional advice, players stand up, players know their worth and their power. And over that ten years or so it totally changed every area of the contract. People always focus on money but there are so many other parts of the contract, which were often disregarded by different players at the time. That has hugely changed over the years and I'm proud of the role I played in that.

I don't really like confrontation. I'd rather keep everybody happy. To sit in a room in front of these types of people and to fight for what's right, to push the game on even further, took a lot of time and effort. And it wasn't just because I was the captain – I actually wanted to do it. I felt as though I could make changes and I could drive them. I felt a responsibility because of where I had come from and what I'd seen. The standard changed every single year. And I've still got notes and notes from preparing for meetings, speaking to different people, and also leaning on the girls in the leadership group for advice and us finding out from our agents what we could do to push at those barriers. We were all in it together and sharing information made us powerful.

I don't think I'm outspoken, or particularly brave. But I was brave enough to have a conversation. That was the main thing for me. If you see something and it's not right, you say something. I'm so proud that I did that and continued to do what was right for the team. Maybe having an individual commercial contract would have suited me more, because at the time I was being used a lot. But it wasn't about me. It wasn't about the bigger players. We were trying to get parity for the rest of the squad, and for those that were potentially coming into the squad who had a future in the Lionesses. For me, it was all about trying to find that balance, to allow us to be protected but also to make sure all of us had value.

When I started, I didn't really think about it: it didn't seem like there was the potential of having a career in football, and certainly not when my family were having to pay £250 a year subs for me to be able to play for Sunderland.

But, for all the trophies, I think the role I played in moving the game on is one of my biggest achievements.

Things are different in the world today and that's a good thing. It's not just in football or sport in general. If I had a little girl and she didn't want to play football, she could still have a career within football, working on the periphery or in the boardroom, in different roles.

We've been taught to be accepted for who we are, but also that dreams are there to be chased, and I think it's nice.

A lot of people have played an important part in this. Matt would probably play down his role, but he was massive. We wouldn't have had those conversations without his in-depth knowledge about contracts. He gave us the ability to have some sort of comparison with what the men were getting. That first £100 for *Match of the Day* was an absolute bonus for me, but I didn't know that X, Y and Z were getting paid a grand for the same appearance.

Both Matt and the PFA opened my eyes to what we

could get to and where the game could go. And not just for me on a personal level, but for England players, for clubs.

But it's not about take, take, take all the time, it's about the changes that needed to happen. For example, there are maternity rights in contracts now. We didn't have any of that when we started, which is crazy. If I'd fallen pregnant I would not have had any protection, I would have had no income whatsoever. Whereas now we can have a career and have a family at the same time. That's massive for females – and why was it never there in the first place? So, in so many different ways, that little flat white that I had in Costa with Matt changed my life dramatically for the better.

The other day I did an appearance and I got six grand for an hour. That's ridiculous. I still think, Who would want me to come and speak to them, let alone pay me that much? But that's where we've come to.

My first annual salary with Arsenal wasn't worth much more than that, so to get that for an hour is crazy. But it didn't just happen. You have to work hard to get to that point. You have to have value and you have to have a profile, which I'm very, very grateful for.

The opportunity is now there. We had to change companies' and brands' mindsets on how they see us as female athletes. It's unbelievable in terms of all the brands that the girls are working with now. There are probably more female footballers on TV than male ones at the moment, in terms of adverts and everything else. And that's because we challenge people and we are ambitious. These are people that can go and do something really good in the sport.

Sometimes it felt like we were hitting our heads against a brick wall. It got frustrating and you felt like you were always trying to justify yourself. But the leadership groups were a great help. If I was ready to quit or if I was pissed off, someone else would be positive and we'd regroup and go again. The PFA were unbelievable in helping us and giving us options. And I think we did find strength in numbers, which was the best thing, really.

It was important that we all stood together, and that first big meeting at St George's Park was really a stepping stone towards what was to come.

RED PHIL

We knew that Phil Neville was going to be the next England coach because he started following us all on Instagram before it was announced.

The notifications started dropping and we were all messaging each other. He'd never managed in women's football before but obviously he was a big name in the men's game, having played for Manchester United, Everton and England, and we were all pretty excited about it.

There were also rumours he'd been going around watching us play for our clubs.

Personally, I was really pleased. I knew he'd won the treble with United in 1999, and all Ste's family are Everton supporters and they liked him.

We were in the annual camp in La Manga in January 2018, and Phil held a big meeting and introduced himself. It was a relief to get it sorted really, after Mark Sampson had left, but I didn't know what it meant for me, whether he'd be giving the captaincy to someone else.

He came over and sat with us at dinner, I think it was me and Lucy, and we were just chatting. He was trying to find out everything, and he talked about what he wanted to bring to the team, which was discipline, hard work and that winning mentality – a lot of what he'd learned at United.

As a football fan, I thought that would be amazing. If he could kind of do the same with us as he'd achieved at United, that would be unbelievable.

After dinner, Casey Stoney messaged me and asked to meet me outside my apartment. At the time she was doing a bit of coaching as well as being a player, so was a bit in-between.

I thought it seemed a bit weird. But anyway, I went out and I could see Phil and Casey walking down the massive steps towards me. Phil had told everyone that he wanted to be called boss because that's what they called Sir Alex Ferguson at United. It wasn't 'gaffer' it was 'boss'. So I said, 'Is everything OK, boss?'

He told me everything was fine and that he wanted me to be captain. He said, 'Chill out, relax, you're my captain.' For me that was a massive moment, because Casey, who I'd replaced, was there. It seemed really respectful and I really, really appreciate Casey for that.

For the rest of the trip, I was able to just relax and look forward to what was to come. Phil had shown that, in terms of the human side, he was very, very good at knowing what to say and when to say it.

At that first meeting he told us that we needed to be on time and respectful above all else. He wanted us to enjoy being on the grass and to work hard. I guess it sounds really simple, but it was really effective because the last three or four months, and the change of management, had been really hard for us as a team. He stripped everything back, got us back to basics and outlined what he wanted. It was like a reset, really, and we needed that.

The elephant in the room was that he hadn't worked in women's football, but he addressed that straight away. He told us that he just saw it as football. He felt he had the experience that was needed.

Phil had been assistant manager to his brother, Gary, at Valencia, which wasn't a success, and we didn't want a repeat of that, but my first impressions were all good – though we didn't get off to the best start.

I injured my ankle and missed the next camp, and I think Phil would probably agree that our first six months as a captain and manager weren't great. I didn't really feel a connection with him and that was mainly because I missed that camp, which was a chance go away, spend fourteen days together, and learn how he works. I didn't show my best football in those first few months. But we got to know each other. I began to know what he expected. And his style of play was very attacking, but very technical too. He wanted us to be ruthless and to win. The way he coached was very energetic and his sessions were intense.

He was also huge on fitness. That was one thing we could control. Other teams might have their strengths, but there was no excuse for anyone to be fitter than we were.

He tried to mirror how he used to train, and he expected us to apply ourselves and do the extras as he had done throughout his career.

To play the way he wanted us to play, we needed to be as fit as we could possibly be, and we worked really hard at that.

He gave me a load of grief for playing for City, given he was a Red. But he was a regular at our place. He used to come and watch us train, and he was probably the first England manager I played for who did that. He would make extra effort to keep in touch and get to know you on a personal level, which was how he built trust. And he watched us play a lot, which was reassuring because obviously there are times when you don't have the best game, and so he was able to build an accurate picture.

We'd finished second again in 2018–19, this time to Arsenal, but I felt like I was playing the best football of my career. Stephen had just been diagnosed and I threw myself into it. We won the League Cup and FA Cup, and again I got to lift the trophy at Wembley, which never gets old.

That season there were so many times when people told

me I didn't have to play because of what had happened with Stephen. But it just made me more determined to win, because winning made those sacrifices worthwhile.

We went to the US for the SheBelieves Cup in 2019 and won it for the first time. I scored against America, a free kick, which is one of my all-time favourite goals. We drew the game 2–2 but beat Japan and Brazil to top the group and it felt like a huge moment for us. For how shit everything was off the pitch, I actually went and excelled more on it. I needed that rhythm and I just churned out performances as we went. I didn't want to miss a game.

Nick Cushing kept asking me if I needed to sit out a game for City. No, I didn't want to. I wanted to play. I wanted to play my best football. And I felt confident that 2019 was probably my best football year in terms of what I produced as a player.

Winning the FA Cup and the League Cup was big. In the League Cup, we went all the way to extra time and beat Arsenal on penalties. I scored one of ours, and that was one of my best games for City. I was defending against Vivianne Miedema, who was in her prime, and we drew 0–0.

What was happening with Stephen gave me perspective, but I was even more driven to do well because I felt I was playing for both of us. Stephen was still coming to the games, and he would help me. He never, ever criticised, but he would always give constructive feedback. Football was my way of coping. I threw myself into it and did every extra training session I could. I did extras when I got home, I got in early to the gym. I would be the last one off the training ground.

In the build-up to the World Cup, Phil was the first England manager to insist that I wasn't going on certain trips. He'd tell me to go home and spend time with Stephen, and not to worry about keeping my place. I didn't have to prove myself to him. I absolutely hated it, not being there, but he was doing the same with the likes of Jill Scott and Kaz Carney, the older players. Looking back on that season, I think that was a big factor in why I played so well, although I'd never have admitted it at the time.

I got my hundredth cap against Sweden, which was an amazing day for me and my family, but all my thoughts were on the World Cup in France.

PENALTY

We had been summoned to a meeting room at St George's Park, and when we opened the door there was a load of people there in military clothing.

They shouted at us. Told us we had twenty minutes to get ready, to leave our phones in our rooms and that we would not be coming back for twenty-four hours.

We were like, what the fuck? Where are we going? I rang Stephen to tell him I wasn't allowed my phone for twenty-four hours. Everyone was rushing around.

We met on the grass outside and these army people told us we were going on a team-building exercise. We did an activity where we were split into teams and had to carry something to a certain place in the quickest time. We camped out for the night and got zero sleep. We were also on rations. It was like a survival task to emphasise team-work and bringing us together. We all had camouflage face paint and army clothes on, and they designed it so you

235

were sharing a tent with someone you probably wouldn't normally share a tent with.

It was all part of the best preparation I'd ever been part of. We worked hard on the pitch, and we also worked hard off the pitch. We brought togetherness to the group, and all the staff were included as well.

We went out to France early and had ten days' preparation. We were based in Nice because two of our group games were there and, obviously, the weather was unbelievable. We got settled in our hotel and we had our own World Cup bus.

All of our families came out and stayed close to us on the promenade, which also helped. I don't think as a group we had been fitter. We'd worked on being sharp and learning what the boss wanted us to do.

We won all of our group games, against Scotland, Argentina and Japan. And we played the maddest game of my life.

We'd prepared for Cameroon, and knew they thrived on chaos. They liked to foul and disrupt. They liked to do mad shit that you would never think of, which makes them difficult to predict.

It was weird from the start. We were sharing a hotel with them, and we tended to keep out of each other's way. Obviously you're trying to keep things secret, your plans and everything, so it was a bit awkward. You'd just keep your head down when you walked past them in the corridor with your tracksuit on.

We had loads of fans in France, which was great, but the Cameroon fans were outside our hotel, playing their music. It was bedlam. You couldn't go out for a coffee.

We played them in a place called Valenciennes, which I won't rush back to. There was nothing there.

I remember the music blaring out when we came out of the hotel to get on the bus. It was all for them. It felt like they were trying to get the better of us before the game had even started.

When it did start, it got weirder. We hadn't been playing long when their goalkeeper picked up a back pass. We got the free kick from about six yards out and they were complaining, asking what they had done wrong.

I'd taken a similar free kick for City against Brighton, but we never, ever practised it. All the girls asked me where I wanted them to be and I just told them to keep out of the way. Anyway, there were eleven of them in the goal. Because of the technique that I have, I was always going to hit it with the inside of my foot and try to curl it and put a bit of swazz on it. I knew there was a little gap in the side, and I knew they would jump, so I was just going to try and hit it low and as hard as I possibly could. It took a deflection, but it went in. My godson and my cousin were at the game, and I could see them celebrating which was amazing.

What followed was the most stop-start game I've ever had. We won 3–0 but they kicked off at two VAR decisions which, in my opinion, were right. At one point they were threatening to walk off the field. That was fine by me. I ran up to the ref and told her to call it off and we'd take the win. Phil gave me an absolute bollocking for doing that.

It deteriorated after half-time. So many fouls. One of their players went right through me, quite high, and I ended up bumping into their manager. He was leaning over me, saying something I didn't understand. I couldn't get up because my ankle was hurting and I remember lying there thinking that this was just madness. By the end I just wanted to get off the pitch. I was happy to get out of there with the win and without being badly injured.

The referee in that game wasn't what we needed. She just couldn't handle any of it. We needed someone strong, but we didn't get that. We were so drained afterwards. I was meant to go out and do an interview, but Phil told me I couldn't and that we were going to play on the injury to my ankle to suggest I wouldn't be fit to play against Norway. I got player of the match, only my second ever in a World Cup, and I can't do the bloody press conference!

We all thought that if we played to the best of our ability we could beat Norway. It felt like this was our time. We were dying for success. We had played together for so long and we knew what Phil wanted from us. We'd seen glimpses, especially against Japan, that we could play that way. Our right-hand side was really strong, and the first goal came after about three minutes from the right with

Lucy crossing for Jill. We started like a house on fire. For that first forty-five minutes, it was probably the best football that we played under Phil and we wiped the floor with Norway. They couldn't really get back, no matter what they threw back at us. The game was pretty much over after an hour.

The US were up next in the semi-final and VAR came to the fore again. It was the first time it had been used at a major tournament and it played a massive role. We had meetings before the World Cup and we knew it would be a big thing, but I don't think anyone realised what was coming. KB was injured and we missed her when they scored to take the lead with a far-post header.

I thought we were playing pretty well, and we deserved the equaliser when Ellen White got it, but they went straight down the other end and scored again, with Alex Morgan doing her famous tea-drinking celebration.

We pushed and pushed, and Ellen equalised in the second half, but it got pulled back for a really tight offside.

Then Ellen got clipped from behind and it was deemed a penalty by VAR. I was never the designated taker for the tournament. Nikita Parris had taken a couple and missed them. There was a big conversation about why Ellen wasn't taking penalties, but Ellen had never taken penalties throughout her career. I don't know why and she's my best mate; I never really got down to the bottom of why she never did.

We took penalties after training, every session, and they'd always get recorded. I'd scored every single one. So after the pre-game meeting, the goalkeeper coach asked me if I'd take a penalty if we got one. I asked if nobody else wanted to do it. He said no, and so I said I would. But I put it to the back of my mind. We weren't going to get a penalty. We'd already had three in the tournament, and I just didn't think we'd get another.

I actually felt confident as I put the ball down. I was having an OK game and I felt quite good. It was just a long wait for VAR.

Did the wait get in my mind? I'm not sure. I knew which way I was going to put it and I knew that I had taken a penalty for City in the Conti Cup final against Arsenal earlier that year and I'd scored it.

I knew I wanted to put it in that same place. I always used to put the ball down, look up at the goal, take two and a half, three steps backwards, look at the keeper and then get my head down. Whereas some people turn away and don't look at the goal when they're walking back, I was always looking and walking backwards.

We had Nike balls then, and I liked to have the Nike logo facing me. I knew which way I wanted the ball to be in that spot. I'd do the same with my free kicks and everything like that. I wanted this penalty to be just like that.

I stepped up and I knew straight away I hadn't got the connection. I just didn't hit it cleanly. I knew it wasn't good enough. I knew before she saved it that it wasn't going in.

The feeling is emptiness. You feel knackered. You're probably running on adrenalin. You're mentally tired and you're playing at nine o'clock at night, and you've done that for four or five weeks now. Your legs just feel heavy. But then I knew I had to get back. Even in the last minutes we were pushing for an equaliser. As a centre-half, I was pretty much playing as a centre midfielder because we'd got them against the wall and we'd changed formation. We were playing three at the back and Millie Bright went up top. Millie then got sent off. If you're going to get sent off for anything, you might as well do it like that, with an incredible challenge. And then the whistle went and it was just utter devastation.

I'm not going to lie and say that I wasn't nervous when I took the penalty. It was our chance to get back into the game with ten minutes left. But there was no doubt. I did not change my mind. I knew exactly where I wanted to put it. I just didn't get enough of a connection. And after that, you're like, Fuck. I've let everybody down. I've let my family down. They've travelled, they've spent all this money to come and watch me play. I knew that it would be hurting them as much as it was me.

Then you think, Why did they choose me? They could have chosen anyone. But that was pretty brief. I was the captain, it was my responsibility. It would have been more of a regret if I hadn't taken it and had put the pressure on a young player instead. There are no regrets. Yes, I fucked it up. I didn't score. But I wouldn't change taking it.

After a game, normally we wouldn't see our families until the next day. But Phil knew that we needed our families, so he said to tell them to come to the hotel, and we could stay up as long as we liked. I wanted to get back and see Ste and my mam and dad, my brother, and just for them to be there because they would make it OK. I couldn't tell you what they said, I probably wasn't listening, but I knew I was safe with them there.

Phil and all the girls were amazing after the game. I was rooming with Ellen, and she was unbelievable. I felt shit for her because she had an unbelievable tournament and she scored goals that got us to that place. And I was thinking, Oh my God, I've let people down. But my focus now was playing in the bronze medal match, because I knew Phil would want to rest me. That would be my way of trying to get something back. That next day was hard as well, because you're absolutely knackered. You've had no sleep. You're thinking about what could have been. And you have to recover. You're having to face what's on your phone, the messages.

Social media was a mix. I was the headline because I'd missed the penalty and let people down. And we had been so close, it was difficult to come to terms with.

Phil came over and told me he had someone on the phone for me. It was David Beckham. He had come to the Norway game with his daughter Harper. For my hero to be on the phone, that was amazing. He got sent off against Argentina in the 1998 World Cup and became a hate figure. He felt like he let the country down and he knew how I was feeling.

Becks said, Look, it's happened, you've not done it on purpose. He told me that it was going to be tough over the next few months, but that I should really lean on my team-mates, my family. He said I needed to know what a good footballer I was, how much I'd done for the country so far. I still can't believe that happened now. For him to take the time to phone me at that moment was unbelievable.

But at the time, nothing's going in. Whatever people are saying to you, you're just in your own little world. I think I got out of the hotel for a bit and went for a walk, just to have a breather.

I didn't watch the penalty back until about a year later, and that was only by chance. I hadn't actively gone and looked for it. I knew what it looked like – it was me who missed it. It just popped up on Twitter one day.

I'm OK with it. When I was watching it back I pulled away from the screen a little bit. I was thinking, For fuck's sake. It was probably one of the biggest moments of my career, and for England as well. And I fucked it up. But

I don't think it's good for me to reflect or beat myself up about it, or seek it out. Why would I do it? When it flashed up, I was just like, What can I do? It's happened. I don't know. I didn't intend to miss it. It was just a shit penalty.

HANGOVER

A lot changed after the penalty miss. People's perception of me seemed to be different. The fans, the media, what was being written: it was like I'd played badly, which I hadn't. That time straight after a tournament is always hard as a player because you go from massive highs to the big low of not getting to a final. But I found that, for the rest of my career, there were times when I thought I was unfairly singled out in match reports and given low ratings.

It was also all change in the WSL. Manchester United had come in with a team, which I thought was great for the competition. We played them on the first day of the season at the Etihad and beat them 1–0 in front of more than thirty thousand.

We were top of the league, a point clear of Chelsea, when Covid hit. As Chelsea had played one game less than us, when it was decided the season would be curtailed they won the title on points per game. Unbelievable.

But, all of a sudden, the priority wasn't football. Given Stephen's situation, I felt like I needed to protect him. And if that meant it was just me and him in the house for however long, so be it.

We were both worried. This was a new thing, and we didn't know what it was. I'd go out to the shops with gloves and a mask on. When I got back, I'd clean the plastic bags. Anything that came into the house was sanitised. Looking back, we were being overcautious, but at the time we just didn't know.

Covid was tough. We're really close to our families and not being able to see them was awful. It also removed our support network. At the time, Stephen was absolutely fine, he was independent and able to do everything. He would normally come to the pitch with me while I was doing my sessions, just to get out the house. But we would never be mixing with other people. We were just in our own little bubble. It was scary, but I think we coped with it really, really well because we're quite routine people anyway.

Because I was captain of City, I'd be in the captain's meetings to discuss what they were going to do. I didn't want them to make the call, but I knew time was running out and they had to do it. We lost by a decimal point. We drew 3–3 with Chelsea on the final day. And it was never a 3–3 game. We played so well. It was devastating that we didn't win, because I really do feel that as the season went on we would have finished the job. Then Nick Cushing left and attention switched to who was going to come in next.

I was gutted when I heard Nick was going to City's club in New York, because I'd just signed a new deal and he was a big part of my decision. He had been by far the best manager I'd ever worked under in terms of getting the best out of me and in terms of my football. He did so much for me in my career. But while I was disappointed, I knew it was an incredible opportunity for him to go to New York and coach men's football. To go there from where he'd come from was unbelievable.

Gav Makel had thrown a few names at me when discussing what route we should go down next. There were two options: either get someone from abroad, like from a Wolfsburg, a Bayern or a Lyon, those types of clubs, or we appoint from within. I thought it might be a good idea to go outside, just to change it up a little bit. But Gareth Taylor, who was coaching lads in the City academy, was mentioned a few times. And then I saw him at the training ground, and he asked me if I thought he should go for the job. I told him it would be different, managing a bunch of girls compared to boys. We will ask why all the time. Any question, we'll ask why. Why do I have to do that? Whereas lads will just get on with it.

Gaz got the job, and our first meeting was on Zoom thanks to the pandemic. We brought in new players and

Lucy Bronze came back, but we finished behind Chelsea again.

Gaz was less fluid than Nick. He wanted certain patterns; he wanted directional play. Considering we'd missed three or four months of football, I don't think we did too bad, actually. But to lose by two points was hard. We lost 1–0 at home to Brighton. That's what cost us the league. There's so little room for error.

Playing behind closed doors was strange. We played Chelsea in the Community Shield at Wembley and there was nobody there. It was like, What the fuck is going on? It felt like an in-house game at the home of football. Even though we were playing big games, it was really difficult to get up for them. It was just a weird sensation.

For training, we'd come in in fives and train on a certain part of the pitch, and you weren't allowed to go on a different part of the pitch. But to be fair, I've never, ever been as fit as I was during lockdown because I threw myself into it. Dawn Scott, the England sports scientist, gave us an unreal programme and told us we were going to use Covid to get stronger than we'd ever been.

At this stage the plan was still to get to the 2021 Euros, which I thought we had a real chance of winning, and then I'd be done.

Me and Ste were like, what else would there be to achieve? I'd won pretty much every trophy at club level bar the Champions League. The Euros got delayed and the

Olympics got delayed so I committed to another two years. Fitness was never an issue, or the ability to compete. And the fact that I played centre-half always helped. After those two years, we can start a family. I can do what I want to do, and Stephen and I can do what we want to do.

With England, there was a massive hangover after the World Cup. We lost something like seven of the next eleven matches and there was a lot of talk about Phil's future. One of those games was a defeat to Germany at Wembley, in front of nearly eighty thousand, which was really disappointing. In January 2021 Phil left to go and manage Inter Miami, and it meant we would need a new coach for the Olympics, as he was going to lead Team GB. There had been a lot of talk about the Dutch coach, Sarina Wiegman, coming in, but they went for an interim for the Games, the Norwegian Hege Riise.

I was desperate to go to the Olympics. You want to be playing big tournaments and we had missed a lot of football over the last year because of Covid. And England had got Team GB the qualifying place because we finished in the top four at the World Cup.

There were still intense Covid restrictions. Tokyo is a beautiful city, but we couldn't see any of it. We couldn't do anything, couldn't go out. We were only allowed out to train; we had to be in our rooms the rest of the time. Me and Ellen had a security guard outside our door the whole time, stopping us from leaving. There was no freedom and it was a sacrifice we had to make to be a part of the Games, but that was not OK. We were in our own hotel away from the Team GB facility. We weren't anywhere near any of the athletes in the Olympic Village. It was just us in this bubble.

We had zero fresh air apart from when we were training. It felt like being in prison. The hotel was fine, but the rooms were tiny. We felt claustrophobic a lot. I don't know how we did it, to be honest. Playing in that Olympics was probably what got us through. It was even harder because we were in a different time zone, eight hours ahead of our families. It wasn't as if we could pass the time by speaking to people. Most people are either in bed, or when we go to bed they're still working or whatever. So I think people found that tough, because normally that's what breaks it up a little bit. The highlight of the day was if one of the security guards had managed to sneak us all in a Starbucks. Ridiculous.

We got to the quarter-final and lost a crazy game to Australia 4–3 after extra time. We were a minute away from going through but Sam Kerr, who is incredible, equalised. Ellen White scored a hat trick, but it was in vain.

That was one of the most humid games I have ever played in. And I got drug tested afterwards and had to sit for four hours in a room on my own. It was a pretty fitting end.

There are tournaments that I've been devastated to be coming home from, but this wasn't one of them. The build-up didn't feel the same, and we weren't playing in front of anyone. We had to fly to Japan with masks on the whole time. I was gutted that we got beaten the way that we did, but it was nowhere near the feeling I had when we lost in a World Cup or Euros.

There was none of that Olympics experience which we had enjoyed in 2012. The only time we went into the village was when we made our way back to Tokyo after we had been knocked out. By then, we'd had enough. We just wanted to get home.

ESCAPE FROM ST GEORGE'S

Sarina Wiegman was made England manager in September 2021, and I was excited about it. I thought this could be the appointment we'd been waiting for as a team. The likes of me, Jill Scott, Ellen White, Lucy Bronze, Demi Stokes, Keira Walsh and Georgia Stanway were the mainstays of the squad and had been playing together for a long period of time. We had no excuses now. We all had tournament experience, the World Cup, the Olympics. The next thing was the Euros. Could we actually go and do it? And there was Sarina's track record: she's won the Euros, she's done well in the World Cup. I liked the way her Netherlands team played. It was similar to what we did. I thought this could finally be a team that could win a trophy for the country.

The first squad got announced and I hadn't spoken to Sarina yet. We were staying at the hotel at Hampshire's cricket ground down in Southampton. After dinner she asked me if I'd mind coming to meet her and the assistant coach for a chat.

She told me that I was going be a big part of the team. She also asked me about Stephen and that situation. I told her that he was my priority. Whatever happens with football, it has to be him before anything. I wanted to get that across to her because I needed her to realise that my circumstances might be a little bit different. She told me she didn't know which way she was going to go with the captaincy, but it would be me for the next few fixtures. I thought that was fair enough.

She wasn't giving much away. I find that hard to deal with, but at the same time, I know that as a manager you want to keep your cards close to your chest. It motivated me to go and train well and to impress. And it didn't really change the way that I was with the girls. I was just going to do what I normally would.

In training, Sarina was trying to put a marker down in terms of tactics, the way that she wanted to play, what she expected. The day before our first match, I did the press conference with Sarina, and it was uncomfortable when I was getting asked questions about the captaincy.

It was just a little bit awkward because I was like, I don't know if this is a question for me, it's more for Sarina.

After the press conference we went to the final training session at St Mary's Stadium, and as usual Sarina ended it with a bit of five-a-side. I made a run forward and then went to come back, and literally as I stepped all I could feel was my foot slipping in my boot.

It was a weird feeling. I went to see the doctor and we both knew something wasn't right.

We went back to the hotel, and I got an ultrasound scan. The doctor said he thought he could see something and that I was going to have to go home. I was devastated and wondering how this was going to impact on everything, because if I miss games there are other people who've got a chance to impress. It's a new squad, it's a new manager. So many things were going through my head.

That six-hour drive up to Manchester wasn't nice at all. I was thinking, Why is it always in the important moments that this happens? Just give me a break.

I don't know what else I could do. I do everything properly, I don't cut corners. I look after my body, eat properly, all that stuff.

The next day I got another scan. It was a tear in my Achilles, so City booked me a specialist appointment down in London. They said I'd be out for around eight to twelve weeks, which would be the end of November.

I got an injection to help it heal quicker. But I was in a boot for six to seven weeks and rehab was tough. It didn't help that we weren't massively staffed at City at the time, and we had a lot of injuries that season. Six or seven big players were out at the same time, and it wasn't anybody's fault but there just wasn't the intense rehab there should have been.

I was back in training towards the end of December. I played some games for City, but just didn't feel right, even though I'd played well. I spoke to a doctor at England, and I spoke to another specialist again. They told me to shut down again for two weeks and then I started panicking because I didn't want another two weeks of not being picked.

I was always checking in and wishing the girls and the manager good luck, but I was a little bit detached from it all, which was hard to take.

I remember having the call with specialists, and then the call with the England doctor and I had a call with Sarina, who told me I was playing well and that she really wanted me to be part of the team. That was reassuring but my foot just wasn't getting better. I couldn't even walk properly.

I went down to London. The specialist said, I think we need to operate, because it's not healed as much as we would have liked it to. I went down with Stephen, and I didn't know what I was going to be waking up to. It could be a cast, it could be a boot. I was dreading it being a cast because I knew we'd need help at home. It wasn't just about looking after me, it was about looking after us both. And I woke up in a cast.

This white thing. It was a pain in the arse. The surgeon told me he's fixed it. He said he'd taken a little bit of bone from my ankle. I would be in the cast for two weeks, just to keep my foot pointed, then it would be stitches out and a boot. I wasn't allowed to do any work because he didn't

256

want me sweating. The operation was on 21 February and the first camp for the Euros was usually around the start of June. I had a six-month injury and I needed to find a way to be fit in three.

I messaged Matt Radcliffe, a physio in Crewe that Stephen had worked with. He said we could do it. That it would be tough, but we could do it.

City were happy for me to give it a try, but then I needed to speak to England to see if it was actually worth it. We went to St George's Park and met them. They were on board.

Matt and I tried everything. I was on the exercise bike with the boot strapped to the pedal. We even found a way for me to do squats with it on. We went back to St George's and met Sarina, the doctor and the strength and conditioning guy.

Sarina said she would need to see me reaching a certain level by the time the camp came around.

She knew I was out for the season and she knew I wasn't going to be able to play any matches. She knew the situation. I was never going to get back to City before the end of the season, but the extra month to June gave us a bit more leeway.

So that was the plan. And every six weeks we would check in. By then, though, I knew that I wasn't captain any more.

On a rare weekend off, Stephen and I went to Rudding

Park, a spa and golf resort in Harrogate. It was kind of a mini-celebration because on the Tuesday I was going to see the surgeon in London, get the boot off and get the all clear to start working again.

We had a lovely night on the Friday, and I was in the spa on Saturday morning when I got a text from Sarina. She called and I told her the boot was coming off on Tuesday. She invited me to watch the girls train and have dinner that day, but I told her I just couldn't miss the appointment. She then said she needed to tell me something. I was no longer going to be captain of the team. She said Leah Williamson had done a really good job, and that she wanted to go in a different direction and obviously I'd not been fit.

I was upset that I'd found out over the phone. For me, that's a face-to-face conversation.

I kind of knew it was coming and I understood why it was coming. It was never, ever anything against Leah, because we got on really well and you could see that she was going to be captain one day. I was devastated, but I couldn't do anything. It's not as if I played my way out. It was just circumstance.

Darbs was great. He's so logical, and he was just like, OK, there's no pressure now. You just have to look after yourself. You don't have to think about anybody else. Now you can just focus on what you need to do.

I was gutted, because I'd had eight years of being captain, and that's a long time. I felt, in that moment, that she wasn't having me. I got that impression. I like to think I read people quite well. Sarina never really gave much away, but I just had a feeling that that was the way it was going to go. I just felt more gutted because it's the best thing I've ever had a chance to do and it's not ended on my terms. It's been taken away from me, and I put so much work into it as well.

I had a little cry and Stephen was like, come on, let's get up, let's get going. You knew this was probably going to happen, and now we can look forward, and now we can get you right. And it doesn't change much in the sense of what you're doing rehab wise.

Sarina had also asked me to keep checking in and to keep coming down. I kept them posted with milestones: when I was out of the boot, when I could jog, when I was on the pitch, kicking a ball again.

Spending all that time doing rehab in Crewe had been a big call, because it's an hour away from me. I'd leave at 9 a.m. and some days I wouldn't get home until 6 p.m. And I was going six days a week, six days a week when I was not really seeing Stephen. Even during my recovery days, I was going down there because I needed to get treatment. I was worried about it, but the prize at the end was so important and we both knew it was the right thing for me to do.

I was running by ten, eleven weeks and they'd said fourteen to sixteen. I was getting to milestones quicker than we ever imagined. We knew there was a risk that my Achilles could go again. We knew that we were pushing boundaries all the time and I was training through a little bit of pain at times, though I was always going to get that with what I'd had. But when there is something you want so much, you just get through it and push through all the boundaries that you think you have as a person and as a player. I did everything I possibly could.

As I was progressing, a few girls had knocks. After the season, there were a few weeks where people could go and train at St George's Park to get ready for the camp. So we moved there so Sarina could see how I was doing. That went well, and it was a week before the next camp when she told me I'd made the provisional thirty for the Euros.

I was made up. I was like, Matt, we did it! We're in the squad! But we still needed to keep working.

I can remember driving to St George's for the first day of camp. Normally I am excited about going there and what's to come, but this time it felt weird, because I didn't really know where I stood. I'd not been part of the team for a long time. I wasn't clear on how the management felt about me and where I would sit in the squad. At the back of my mind, I didn't think they would let me push all this way, putting my body at risk, if I wasn't going to go to the tournament.

I gradually got eased back in and I was feeling OK. I wouldn't say I was 100 per cent, but I would have got there.

A lot of things felt new to me – I actually felt like I was making my debut. The following Wednesday, we were going to find out who was in the final squad. We met up on Monday and had a friendly on the Thursday. We trained Monday, Tuesday, Wednesday. I've never done three days' training in a row, so I wondered how they were going to plan my week. I got called in by the doctor, sports scientist and Sarina and they said I'd train on all three days.

I asked about the game on Thursday and Sarina said, We'll see.

Prince William came to the training session on Wednesday, and we were doing 11 v 11. We then got a message saying that afternoon we'd each be told whether we were in the squad or not. So we were all hanging around.

I went to get a coffee, and then I got a message asking me to go upstairs. I went in and it was just Sarina and the assistant there.

I just knew. I could just tell by their faces. They didn't feel as though I'd had enough game time. I told them they had known I wasn't going to get games. They knew that from the start. It just didn't make any logical sense. Sarina told me she didn't feel as though I was up to the rhythm. I had told her I wasn't going to be up to the rhythm. Anybody that knows anything about football should know that. I told her that was the situation coming in. She said she just didn't feel as though I was going to be able to get into rhythm quick enough.

I was upset, and I was angry. What the fuck? I didn't get how it had come to this point. If she knew I wasn't going to be ready, why didn't she stop me weeks ago?

It still upsets me now because I don't really understand how much clearer we could have been with the plan. We involved Sarina, we involved City. Gaz knew. My doctor at City knew. The specialist knew.

I just walked out. I was fuming. I felt like I got my argument across, although I did get emotional. I think that's just me as a person. I didn't mention Stephen, or the decision to spend so much time away from him, because I think then I would have got really upset.

It got worse. They started to tell us half an hour before the announcement of the full squad. So there was a lot of press there. My first thought was, How the fuck do I get to my car without being seen? How am I going to get all my stuff? I didn't need people seeing me. I just wanted to be by myself. I went back to my room and phoned Ste, and just absolutely sobbed my heart out. I couldn't bring myself to ring Matt Radcliffe, because I felt like I'd let him down. I asked Stephen what to do. He told me to ask security to get my car pulled round to the bottom.

I rang the security woman, Sue, and asked her to get my car to the front. Ellen knocked on my door and I just burst into tears again.

I started to walk out in my England tracksuit, shuffling along the corridor with my case, trying to avoid everyone.

My head was in bits, and I swear I left stuff behind in the room. Trying to sneak out of St George's Park is not good for anybody. I made it to the car, lobbed everything in the boot and drove to a petrol station, because I had no fucking petrol either.

Katie Zelem phoned me; she hadn't been picked either. She was devastated too. We were there for each other over that summer. But that drive home: you know when you sometimes drive, and you don't know how you've got home – it was definitely like that.

My first thought was that I needed to get out of England. My phone was getting peppered. I needed to get away. My head was a bit of a mess. I couldn't believe this was happening. I just felt numb.

We always go on holiday to Ibiza every year, and as soon as I got home, I told Stephen we just needed to go. I wanted my family there. We'd pay. I didn't mind. I was like, we're getting out of here. I got in the house, and I started looking at flights straight away.

We went, but throughout that holiday it was hard to get away from it all because the girls were starting to play group stages and you could feel the buzz back home. I got asked to do BBC punditry and I turned it down. I didn't really feel as though I could comment on games as a current England player.

We were in Ibiza for about ten days. For the first four it

was just me and Stephen and it was still quite raw. It was hard, because I was lying there on the sunbed in the amazing sun, at an amazing hotel, but I couldn't help but think about it. I felt as though I got a bit shafted. That was my initial reaction. I just don't know why it happened that way.

It was hard to switch off, but as the holiday went on I started to relax a little bit.

I got back and I watched most of the games, I couldn't not do. I watched because my mates were playing. I wanted the girls to do well, because it had nothing to do with them. I watched the Spain game, then the semi-final and the final. We went to the Trafford Centre for some reason during the first game of the Euros and it was full of England fans. I was like, Stephen, we should have planned this better, going to the Trafford Centre when England are playing at Old Trafford.

I invited my best friend Sophie, her boyfriend Jake and my godson Alfie over for the final. It was a boiling hot day and Alfie wanted to go to the football field and play. So we went before the game, then came back and watched it. Bloody hell, they put us through the mill, didn't they? I was made up for Chloe Kelly, because she had been fighting to get back into the squad as well after her knee injury. To see them win was lovely. But it was a bit of a weird feeling, I'm not going to lie. I was absolutely buzzing that we'd won and I was happy for my teammates, but obviously a part of me wished I could have been there, especially after all the tournaments I'd been to. But you can't live life like that, can you? I messaged my mates, and I messaged Leah when she got the captaincy to offer my support. She hasn't done too bad so far, has she?

At no point did I think about retiring. I always said to everybody, I'm never retiring from England. Some players do that. I'm not retiring from England until I retire from football. That's how I always wanted it to be.

OUT AGAIN

I refused to give up on England. Sarina had said I needed game time, so I threw myself into pre-season training with City. The season before, when I was injured for a lot of it, we finished fourth and Gaz was under a bit of pressure. We'd only won one Conti Cup and the FA Cup.

I had a good build-up, and I felt as though I was back enjoying my football, which was probably the most important thing. I felt fit. We played Villa away the first game of the season and lost 4–2. We had players coming in and lots of changes, and we just weren't in sync with each other. We weren't gelling as a team. It took a while to get to where Gaz wanted us to be. After the Villa game we had Chelsea away and lost 2–1. So that was the first two games gone. I'd played in both and done all right but I didn't get picked for the first international camp. I couldn't really argue with that because I'd only played two games. But to be fair, she called me, and I asked her if she saw me as a potential starter. If she did, then I was obviously going to fight for my place.

It was important to get clarity because things were changing with Stephen. If I'm going to go away with England, it needs to be for the right reason. I need to be sure my time there is valuable.

Stephen had stopped driving, which was a big thing, and his hands were getting weaker. He was still able to walk, but he was a little bit shaky in the sense that he wasn't confident enough to go for a walk by himself.

In the house he'd be fine, but going out for a walk was a struggle. He understandably started to worry a little bit about when I was going to training or when I was going away.

I had the conversation with Sarina, and I was told to keep working hard and to get that rhythm. City had brought in a Spanish defender, Laia Aleixandri, and someone told me she was going to start our next game against Leicester. I waited for Gaz to tell me, but I was pissed off I'd heard it from someone else first. Come on, I'm thirty-four. He knew what I'd been through in the summer and had told me he had my back, that he would get me back into the team, but then dropped me at the first opportunity. That's nothing against Laia, because she's an outstanding player. But I felt I deserved more respect.

The team was announced the day before the game, and

I wasn't in it. Gaz then called me. He told me I hadn't got my rhythm yet. Honestly, fucking rhythm. I now hate that word after the last two years of my career. I just don't get it. If I can't get rhythm without playing, how are you helping me by not playing me? Leicester would have been a great game for me to go in and get this rhythm. I'd have loads of the ball. I'd be able to play the passes I wanted to play. But it fell on deaf ears. Up until Christmas, I just never got a chance to get back in.

I got an opportunity by default because we had injuries. I took it and I played so well for City in that last half of the season. But in terms of England, I wasn't given an opportunity to play.

I did everything. Sarina met me in the October and pointed out that I still hadn't had any games. I started to play for City at the end of January. I played against Arsenal at home and had a really good game. We won. And I kept my place for the rest of the season.

By the April camp I'd played ten games at a high level. I was offered another year at City, and it was going so well that I signed. At the time, Gaz told me it was the best football I had played in my career. I was so focused on keeping my place and I had high hopes I'd make the England camp. I think everyone expected me to be in the squad, and my teammates were convinced I would be. My hopes were raised because if you weren't in the squad, you usually got a call from the manager before it was announced, and I hadn't had one. No news is good news and all that. But the squad came out and my name wasn't there. I had an email instead, telling me I was on standby.

I called Sarina and told her I was confused. The one thing that she said I'd not got, I've now got. I knew I'd played well. She'd been to some of my games and seen it for herself. And it wasn't like I was just performing against some of the smaller clubs. I'd played against Arsenal, Chelsea, where we beat them both at home, and played well against United, who were becoming a force. Games where I was coming up against strikers that we would probably face in the World Cup. She responded by saying she just didn't feel she could take anyone out of the squad for me. It felt like she'd moved the goalposts.

What else can I do? I couldn't do this any more. I realised I just wasn't in her plans. The end of the season came. We finished fourth and didn't win a trophy, but I was happy with how the last half of the season had gone.

For the first time in my career I felt like nobody had my back. Nobody who would stick with me or trust me.

I got an email telling me I was on standby for the World Cup, which was in Australia, and that I needed to fill a load of forms in for my visa.

I asked Gaz if he'd spoken to Sarina and he hadn't. I thought that was strange, because if I was going to go you'd expect your manager to be asked for his opinion.

I filled out the forms and we were told we'd know the final squad the following Tuesday. On the Monday I had an appearance at St George's for Nike. When I went back to the changing room afterwards, I had a missed call from Sarina. She didn't know I was there, so when I told her she asked me to go and meet her in the canteen, where she told me she wasn't taking me. I kind of had a feeling anyway, because I'd had no communication since I phoned her in April. And I'm not stupid. I'm old enough to know that if you've not been involved in the last few months, it's very rare to just come in randomly to the World Cup squad.

She told me they had a few worries about when I changed direction and the ball came over the top. She also said when I pressed and came back out, I was a little too reactive. It felt like a complicated way of telling me they didn't feel I was quick enough. I read it, rightly or wrongly, as I was too old. At that moment I was just sick of fighting.

I mean, what else could I do? She asked me to play games. I played games. She asked me to compete against big players and in big games. I'd done that.

And it wasn't just as a player. I felt like I had other attributes that could help the group in the World Cup. It wasn't as if I expected to play every game. I knew that if I'd be part of the squad, I'd be the person that would be supporting the others.

I also found myself wondering if this would have been a face-to-face conversation if I hadn't already been at St

George's. Sarina told me that I probably wouldn't play for England while she was in charge. I think she would have much preferred it if I had retired there and then, but there was no chance. The whole thing felt pretty brutal.

I put my points across. I said I couldn't change her opinion, but I did feel as though I could bring something different to the group. Experience, leadership. I felt as though I was still a good player and that I'd been to these tournaments before and could be valuable.

She'd obviously made her mind up, which is fine, and I've got to respect that to a point. The problem was more that I think she'd intended to have this conversation over the phone, and she knew she was going to tell me I wasn't in her plans at all. I thought that called for a face-to-face conversation given the career I'd had.

I just wished her luck, walked out of the door and went home.

At least this time I didn't have to sneak out. And when I got to my car there was petrol in it.

The journey home was easier. The thing was out of my hands. Sarina just wasn't having me, no matter what I did. I felt some peace with that. I'd done what I'd been asked. There was just no changing her opinion. I guess the biggest disappointment was that I had allowed myself to have some hope, but then I'd always had a feeling that it wasn't going to happen.

I was gutted that I didn't think I'd play for England again. Playing for England is the greatest honour you can ever get. To have my last game against the Republic of Ireland behind closed doors at St George's Park just didn't seem right.

I'd pictured a proper send-off. A chance to do it properly. If you look at the way Jill Scott and Ellen White bowed out, at Wembley, winning the Euros, it couldn't be more perfect than that, and they both totally deserved that moment.

I didn't get that opportunity or even the opportunity to prove people wrong. It was never going to happen. In terms of emotion, I was less upset than when I didn't make the squad for the Euros.

Despite having a contract for another year, I wasn't sure if I was going to continue playing. But because I'd ended the season really well, I thought let's try one more. I wanted reassurance that I'd still have a big role to play, because I didn't really want to be sitting on the bench.

We had four centre-halfs at City fighting for two spots, but it was healthy competition. It didn't change how we were with each other. It was always trying to bring out the best in each other, trying to fight as much as we can.

Gaz and the sporting director Nils Nielsen told me I might not be starting a lot, but I had a role to play in terms of being a leader and looking after the younger players.

I'm stubborn, and I decided I wanted to play the full season. I felt like I had a point to prove, and I knew that deep down I could do it. I had no injury problems whatsoever and I was fresh. I knew it was going to be my last contract and it would take me to ten years with City, so I threw myself into pre-season.

THE END

It's 19 November 2023, we're playing Manchester United in front of forty-three thousand at Old Trafford, we're winning 3–1 and I've never wanted to go on a football pitch less in my life.

I hadn't been getting picked for City and I'd not played any league football for more than a month, and even then it was a few minutes when we were beating Bristol City 5–0 at home.

I'd just returned to the dugout from escorting Laia Aleixandri to the changing room after she got sent off. She'd been punching the walls and I'd been trying to calm her down.

When I got back to the bench, Gareth Taylor told me to get warmed up. I was stunned. It didn't make sense. We'd played Chelsea at home previously, had two players sent off when we were winning 1–0 and I was desperate to come on and help us see it out. He wasn't, and we'd ended up conceding in the sixth minute of injury time.

I took my jumper off, took my trousers off. I don't think I've ever doubted myself more than in that moment. It was the worst I'd ever felt going into a game. We were winning 3–1 and all I could think about was what would happen if I came on and we conceded twice. There was still plenty of time left.

I asked Gaz where he wanted me to play. He asked me where I wanted to play, which I'd not had before. I told him just to put me in the middle of defence. I went on for fifteen minutes, organised things and we were able to keep our lead. But that was a feeling I'd never had before going on and I never wanted to experience it again.

For all my experience, for all the big games I played in, that was the worst I'd felt.

My dad and brother told me later that they felt the same, that they were so nervous. It wasn't because they weren't confident, but I'd been battered down so many times over the last eighteen months they didn't know what impact that might have had.

You start doubting yourself. I know that I'm a good player, but in that moment I was worried.

Afterwards I just thought, I can't do this every week. Why should I be wasting so much energy worrying about how I'm going to play a game that I've played since I was four or five? I felt valued because I helped us get the win, but didn't feel there was trust in me to go and do what I needed to do.

I didn't really get the chance I thought I deserved, and my last season was probably my hardest. I would play in just the cup games. I'd play well in them, but it would never follow on to anything else.

The manager was set on his back four and I wasn't in it. When we had injuries, he would shift everyone around and not pick me.

I accepted it and vowed to be the best person that I could be on the bench, be the team's biggest supporter, be there for the girls. If I couldn't add something on the pitch, I needed to do something away from the pitch. That was my thought process throughout the whole of the season. This is not me being fake. I can only influence what I can influence.

In one of the games, when the manager brought someone else on to play centre-half, it dawned on me that I was now fourth choice. I was sitting on the bench thinking, How the hell has it got to this point?

I spoke to Nils, and asked him if I was going to ever get a chance.

I just didn't know what I was getting out of it any more. In the October we had an international break and we had six days off, so I went to Abu Dhabi to do City's coaching clinics, something I'd done on and off since 2015.

Stephen had his walker by this stage, and he was going to come with me. But on the morning we were due to go he had a fall and ended up in hospital. That changed things. It knocked his confidence and he started to rely on me a lot more.

Now I was not only dealing with football, my whole schedule and my routine at home had massively changed. I was mentally and physically exhausted for about two months. I was so tired and drained because you just get on with it. We just kept adapting as we went. My only vice was getting out and playing football, but I wasn't able to do that because I wasn't being picked. I was just training for nothing. I was coming home absolutely knackered, but I needed the energy to help Stephen.

At home he needed help up the stairs sometimes, help getting dry when he comes out of the shower, putting his clothes on. Little things you probably take for granted.

Mentally, it took its toll on both of us. We never really spoke about it. It was just something we had to do.

When I'm tired, I'm a bit of a mardy bitch, so I was thinking something had to give at some point. We either had to change what we were doing or something had to change with what I was doing. Stephen told me to give it a think over Christmas, because we had two weeks off, which was great. We got to go home and see the family. I was still doing my training but I just never had the buzz of wanting to go back to City after the break. Normally I'm dying to get back in, but I just didn't really have that drive.

Nothing was going to change. I'd spoken to the sporting director. Matt had also spoken to him about me maybe retiring over Christmas. He said he'd hate it if I stopped and we won the league, and I missed the chance to go out the right way.

As the weeks went on, I was probably getting twenty minutes here and there, and in games where I maybe should have come on I wasn't being used.

Even though I felt like that, I know that the team really appreciated what I did for them. But my mind was made up that this was going to be it.

We deliberated over when we would announce it. We finally decided to do it in April, so people would know before the season finished. I went in to do my announcement interview with City. That was the only time I really got upset, because I went in and it was just all old pictures of me playing for City on this big screen. I wasn't prepared for that. I was prepared for the actual interview, but seeing that stuff made me realise it had come to an end. It dawned on me that there had been so many amazing memories here, that we'd done something special. It was tough.

We also had a meeting with the general manager about what my role was going to be after football. So it was kind of a perfect day, in a way, because I was in a privileged position that not many retired footballers get, to have something ready for you when you're finished. I put a post out on social media, a statement I'd prepared with Matt, and I'd never felt lighter in the last two years.

I was at home when I pressed send. We didn't want the news to get it out. We wanted it to be me announcing it. I messaged my teammates ten minutes before I put the post out. Telling them was probably the hardest thing, because it made it final.

I told them I'd been thinking about it for a while, but I'd come to the decision to finish. I said I'd give it everything until the end of the season to make sure we won the league. They were the first people to know apart from my family. And then obviously I sent the statement out on social media and cried for the next two hours.

My phone immediately lit up. I just had to put it down. It was impossible for me to reply to people there and then because it was important that me and Stephen were together. I was with him, Sky News was on, I was on the yellow ticker and all my interview stuff was coming on.

After that two hours, I started replying to people. I had training the next day and I made sure I was first in. As me and Stephen say, just keep things normal, right? Gaz embarrassed me in the team meeting, which I'd told him not to. I didn't want anything said in the meeting. I just wanted to be normal.

He put it on the big screen and stuff, which meant a lot, to know that people appreciate what you've done for the club and for other people. It was nice, but my mindset was just to enjoy the last six weeks of playing football and training, and being with those people. The relief washed over me.

So many people reached out to me. Old managers, old teammates, people from school. Opponents, rivals. I was grateful to be able to do things on my terms. England put something on Instagram. I had no message from Sarina. To be fair, I probably caught England a little cold. In a perfect world it should have been a joint thing between me, City and England. But they had hardly spoken to me for two years, so why should I involve them? Where had they been?

We were confident that we were going to win the title for the first time since 2016. The first game after my announcement was against Liverpool away, and I got the most amazing reception from both sets of fans. I got goosebumps. It just reassured me that people understood not just what I'd done for City but for women's football.

Our last home match was against Arsenal, and we were winning 1–0 with a minute left. A point would have kept the title in our hands, but we conceded twice and ended up losing, and the next week Chelsea won the league on goal difference. I was absolutely fuming, but what City did for me and my family afterwards was incredible.

I was on a massive downer because of what had happened, but I had to go out and say goodbye. I didn't really get emotional. I'd done my crying on the way in. I cried from the moment I got in my car until I got to the ground. When I got there Chloe Kelly banged on my window. I had to ask her for a minute. She gave me a hug and told me to get it all out.

The result killed me, but fifty of my friends and family had come down to see me. We spent an hour on the pitch. All my nephews, my godchildren, we just played football on the pitch for ages, me and my crew. I didn't really want to leave. There's a shot of us all in front of the goal, which I have as my WhatsApp picture.

BEYOND FOOTBALL

Pep Guardiola arrived in 2016 to manage the men's team, and I had been there for his unveiling, which was huge. Our paths crossed over the years, but I remember one day I had to go to the men's side of the building to use a machine they had in the gym. The receptionist came in and told me Pep wanted to see me. Because I knew her, I thought she was taking the piss. She was adamant that she wasn't, and that I had to go to his office.

I didn't even know where his office was. She had to tell me. I went up and knocked on his door, and he invited me in. There was a tactics board in there, with the instructions for the next game, which was against Everton, and a load of family photos. I couldn't really believe I was in there. He said he was reaching out to see how I was, how things were over on the women's side, and he said he'd watched us the other day and I'd played really well. He then asked me if I'd ever thought about being a coach or a manager. I told him I wasn't really sure, and he said that I had to do it. He said he could see me being that and I just thought, Well, if Pep Guardiola, one of the best managers there's ever been, thinks that, then I'd better start doing my coaching badges.

He also asked me how Stephen was doing, which meant a lot. For him to know his name, it was really personal. We then had a chat about the upcoming game, which was the next day, and ran through what the men were going to do and how they were going to approach it. He asked for my opinion, and I didn't really know what to say because he's the best in the world.

He also said if I ever need any help his door was open. Just before I retired, we were training and he came to watch. The levels went through the roof! He asked me to come over and he congratulated me on my retirement. For everything he has won, he is such a humble and normal person. He said again, if I needed him, he was always there.

I told him I was doing my coaching badges and he invited me to come and study what they did next season. 'Come with me and learn,' he said. How do you say no to that? So while I can't tell you how this next year will look, that's definitely something I will be doing.

I'm often asked what I'm going to do next. You look at people like my old friend Jill Scott, who's doing everything and was even Queen of the Jungle, but I'm not sure that will be me!

It's a bit scary, isn't it? I've been told to keep my options open for as long as I possibly can. But, honestly, I still don't really know what I want to do. I know I've got opportunities, so it's for me to embrace them and try different things, because all I've known is a pitch and a ball.

I'll 1,000,000 per cent take Pep up on his offer. Even if I don't go into coaching, to be able to watch him at close quarters and feel part of it is something you have to do.

I've done newspaper columns and punditry, which is an option, and I do like the idea of being a sporting director one day.

I'm doing my A Licence, which hopefully I'll complete this year. If I do go down the coaching route I'd want to learn from a senior coach, assist and find my way. Whether that's in the men's or women's game, it doesn't really matter, to be honest.

My perfect job would be Man City manager. City are all I've known for ten years and probably all I'll know for the next few. I played for them 242 times, won four Conti Cups, three FA Cups and a WSL title, and it would be nice to add some more to that. The women's team are moving to a new purpose-built training ground and they're naming a pitch after me there, and there's also going to be a mosaic of my career.

Managing City would be the ideal scenario, but we'll see. Then England? Who knows.

What I can guarantee is that my team would play with

passion and wear their hearts on their sleeves, but also be technically really good. And defensively solid.

I wouldn't limit myself to just coaching on the women's side. On my A Licence training, we coached a girls' team on the first day and then an Under 18s lads' team. I was a bit nervous, as a female coming in, but the feedback I had from both groups was the same. I was seeing things and I was letting them know how I could improve them. I think the messaging is the same, whether I'm male or female.

Having kids is a big thing and it's something we're looking forward to. With Stephen's situation it will be hard for us if we have a baby, but we've got a lot of support from our families. Spending more time with my family and also potentially having a family of our own, is something I'm really excited to have. It would be the perfect retirement present, to be honest.

And with Stephen, it's about making the most of every day, keeping things as normal as possible. When Rob Burrow died it was a shock, because we'd seen him a few weeks earlier and he looked really well. We used to call Stephen, Rob and Doddie Weir the Three Amigos, and it hits home that now it's just Stephen.

But I think if we always had that in the back of our minds we wouldn't live properly because we'd just be worrying all the time.

Ste is unbelievable. I thought he'd be really upset when

Rob passed away, which obviously he was, but he never really showed emotion. That's his way of dealing with it. We just keep going. We keep fighting.

There's a lot to enjoy. Last weekend was Matt's wedding, and they went to play golf. Stephen was in the buggy with the lads, taking the piss.

We have a horse, and I've always wanted a dog. I mentioned it during lockdown, but Ste said I wouldn't be able to look after it because I was never in the house. Anyway, his mate Will Buckley, who he played with at Bolton, had a racehorse already and they decided they'd get one together. They went and bought one on my birthday and called it Darbucks, which I thought was because I liked coffee, but it was actually a play on their names.

Our colours are red and blue, because Stephen's a Liverpool fan and Will's an Oldham fan, and he's in a nice stable in Ormskirk, which we visit quite a bit. I'm not going to lie, Darbucks was shit the first year, he didn't win anything, but he's won a few now and it's a great day out to go and watch him racing. I've still not got a dog, mind.

When I think about children, I go back to my own childhood and kicking a ball against the black pole. If I could travel through time to that backyard and speak to that little girl I'd tell her to never stop chasing what you want to do, no matter what that is. And don't worry about what other people think. That would be my biggest thing. Growing up when I did, there were a lot of different perceptions, different challenges to get to where I wanted to go. But maybe instead of worrying I could have put that energy into my football.

If we do have a girl, she will face a lot less barriers than I did. We broke down a lot of those, and that's something I'll always be proud of.

WE'VE COME A LONG WAY

When I was playing at Sunderland, I was buzzing if we were able to train on a decent pitch. It didn't need to be ours, it just needed to be decent. And if we got a place to change, that was a bonus.

Now, clubs have to hit certain criteria to be able to have a centre of excellence. City are moving to a £10 million training facility of their own next year. Young girls have a chance. I'm devastated I won't be able to use that facility. But to have been part of that and know what I've done to help the game get to that point is pretty amazing.

All those tough conversations, all those meetings, have been worthwhile. And it's not just me. A lot of people have driven the game to where it is today.

The game has progressed and is a lot more competitive. We just need to find consistency in everything we do. There's an expectation that when you get into the WSL, you're able to produce a certain size crowd, you're able to attract a number of players, you're able to produce your own home-grown players, you have your own training facilities. If we can get that across a number of leagues, then we can start to mirror the men's game.

We need to attract more fans, but that is growing and will continue.

I have had an amazing career and financially I could not have dreamt of where I ended up. I went from getting men's kit out of a bin bag and buying my own boots to getting free ones from Nike with my name on them. When I first heard about that, I thought they meant like at primary school, when your mam puts your name in the back of your clothes.

The rise from my first contract to my last one is crazy. To go from paying to play to being on the money I was on in the last couple of years at City is difficult to get my head around. Not that I have ever, ever taken it for granted – although I did get a Range Rover! That's probably the only thing we've ever bought that's flashy.

It's the first time I ever had a heated steering wheel, and I miss it now because I only had it for a couple of years.

We're not massive spenders, but there are nice elements to it. If we're going on holiday, we don't have to think about where we are going. If we want to go to Ibiza tomorrow, we can go. We don't have to think about whether we can afford it. And even going shopping or ordering stuff online or going out for food, we don't have to be careful with what we choose.

And that's not just because of me. Stephen worked so hard in his job, and he had an unbelievable football career.

We never were in debt with the wedding, whereas a lot of people have a lot of debt for a long time so we're so grateful, but we've worked hard to be in that position.

The game is unrecognisable now from when I started, but there is still work to be done on changing people's attitudes. The abuse of female pundits is something that makes me pause when I think about going down that route. If I'm going to go into that world, I want to be judged on what I know, not for the fact that I'm a female. Judge me on my football knowledge, the experiences that I've had, rather than the fact that I am a girl.

I have so many great memories to look back on. Captaining my country, winning caps, lifting the FA Cup – there's something about the FA Cup, having watched it growing up on Jamieson Terrace. The Olympics goal against Brazil was the moment my life changed. And I'll never forget driving to the ground after the 2015 World Cup and seeing that young boy with my name on the back of his City shirt. I don't know what the future holds, but I'd hope there will be more memories like these.

I don't really have any regrets, other than caring too much about what other people thought. I had a few chances to go to America, which would have been huge, but being realistic there was no way I could ever be that far away from my family.

I still go home sometimes and go for a run, round the welfare. My uncle runs the cricket club, and as I go past he always calls me in for a drink. My shirt is in the clubhouse and there's a plaque outside. Whenever I go back, people are always asking me how I'm getting on.

I like to think I've done them proud.

ACKNOWLEDGEMENTS

Never in a million years would I have imagined being able to share my story with you all. A girl from the North-East writing an autobiography, who would have thought?

To be able to finally put down in words the last thirty-six years of my life has been therapeutic to say the least, and the most perfect timing a week after I had announced my retirement from the sport I love and the sport that has made the biggest impact in my life.

The process has been intense, emotional but also rewarding.

So here's to trying to make sure I say thanks to everyone who has influenced me and my journey. Firstly, a big thank you to everyone at Little, Brown and David Luxton for giving me the opportunity to share this book with you all; your help and guidance has made this process easy. Mike Keegan, the man with the words, I hope I didn't manage to bore you with our hours of talking. There were certainly plenty of laughs and tears along the way. Thank you for being able to tell my story exactly how I wanted it to be: honest and real.

Let's start back at home, the place that made me: South Hetton. What I love about the village and the people is that everyone gets behind anyone with a dream. Without the support, the love and the positivity from you guys I wouldn't have achieved anything. During a time when girls weren't meant to play football, you accepted me and pushed me all the way. So I hope I made you all proud on my journey and I will never ever forget where I came from.

To represent my clubs, Sunderland, Leeds, Arsenal and Manchester City, and my country, England, was a dream. To my teammates, my managers, the team behind the team and the team behind that team, and the fans that supported me along the way, THANK YOU for making me the person, player and leader I became. So many people have told me that they are the best days of your life, and they are certainly right.

Amy, Lauren, Emma and Sophie, my 'bessies'. Wow, I don't even know where to start. Thank you for always remembering me as 'Stephy from South Hetton' and for being there at my games, arranging our diaries around my schedule for a catch-up, being on the end of the phone or the endless group chats, but also for being my biggest supporters along the way. I love you all and you know how much I love my godsons and goddaughter.

I know you will hate this, Matthew, but hands down none of this would have been possible without you. From that coffee in Manchester, I don't think either of us would have imagined the last thirteen years and how quickly things have changed. I rely on you for anything and everything (apart from the coffee shop choice). I know I tell you this all the time, but you are amazing at your job. You are honest, I can trust you and you always want the best for me and what was and is right for my career. Thanks for the endless phone calls, organising my life and reminding me of my to-do list, but also for representing me and giving me the opportunity to live my dreams. Matty, thank you for always being there no matter what time of day it is and for being one of our closest friends.

I'd like to think that everyone knows how much family means to me. Thank you for always supporting and loving me constantly. To Grandma Doreen for bragging to absolutely everyone that you are my grandma. I think you are more famous than me in women's football. I love you.

To my extended family, Christine and Paul, I couldn't have imagined having a better mother and father-in-law. You really have welcomed me into your family and treated me like your daughter from day one. Kevin and Sue (BIL and SIL), thank you for the laughs, ice cream-gate, the holidays, but most importantly for allowing me to be auntie to Thomas and James, my amazing nephews. I hope, Thomas and James, that you know how much I love you both, and I can't wait to see you grow up and achieve your dreams.

Stuart, bro, my best, best friend. We have been through a lot, but you know what – we have always had each other. I know you're probably sick of being known as 'Steph Houghton's brother' but I want you to know how proud I am to be 'Stuart Houghton's sister'. You are the most amazing man, caring, loyal, kind and funny, and already smashing life. Seeing you get married this summer to Keavney (who is just as amazing as you) was one of the best days of my life, to see how happy you both were. I'm excited to see what the future holds and I am with you all the way.

Mam, thanks for the high pony and the constant matching of scrunchies and giving me the confidence to be anything I wanted to be. Thank you for always being caring, loving, hard-working, sacrificing everything for us in them early days and being able to always take my mind off football. You always know when to give me a mam hug and always know what to say to make things better. You are the most amazing mam, you are beautiful inside and out and I am so proud of everything you have done and continue to do.

Dad, thanks for them long car journeys, the constant pep talks and teaching me how to kick a ball. Thanks, Lenny, for being my biggest-ever supporter, being honest with me, pushing, guiding me and keeping me grounded along the way. I'm so glad we experienced all these amazing moments together and I sure will miss looking to see where you are on game day and you shouting me and the team on from the stands. I always wanted to make you proud with my performances because this wasn't just my career, it was ours, and I love you so much.

Finally, Stephen, my husband, I know I tell you this every day, but you are amazing, everything about you. From the moment I met you, I knew we were meant to be together. No matter what, we are a team, we are strong and we have each other. You are my inspiration. Every day, you make me want to be a better person, friend, daughter and wife because of you. I will always be thankful and grateful that you love me the way that you do, it's the most special feeling in the world. I would do anything and everything for you and for us.

You are my soulmate, my life and a real-life hero. I love you forever and always.